I0560869

DEFEATING THE
PYTHON
SPIRIT

DISCOVER THE SYMPTOMS OF THIS SPIRITS AND HOW IT OPERATES,
CONTAINS DANGEROUS PRAYERS & DECREES TO BREAK FREE
FROM ITS SQUEEZING STRONGHOLD!

PRAYER M. MADUEKE

PRAYER
PUBLICATIONS
UNITED STATES

ISBN: 979-8701638271

Published by Prayer Publications.
Printed in the United States of America.

4 Free Ebooks

In order to say a 'Thank You' for purchasing *Defeating the Python Spirit*, I offer these books to you in appreciation. Click or type maduke.com/free-gift in your browser.

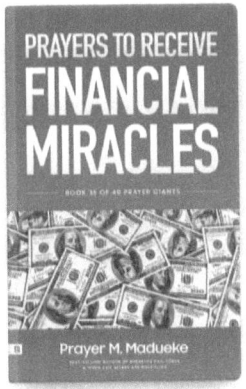

Message from the Author

I want to see you succeed, grow, and break free from negativity and obstacles. My hope is for you to thrive, unaffected by negative influences and challenging situations. Because of that, please permit me to introduce two courses that I believe passionately will help you:

1. To break the evil altars and powers of your father's house, The role of altars in the realm of existence is very key because altars are meeting places between the physical and the spiritual, between the visible and the invisible.

    Unless a man cuts off the evil flow from the power of his father's house, he will not fulfil his destiny. Click here to learn more about my course on how to tear down unholy altars and close the enemy's entryways into your life!

2. To help you seamlessly break iron-like problems, illness, delayed marriage, poverty, or any long-standing battle.

    Discover the transformative power of Christian fasting and prayer. Remember, Matthew 17:21 teaches us, *"But this kind of demon does not go out except by prayer and fasting."* Ready to overcome your struggles? Click here to learn more about this course.

Embrace the journey ahead with faith, for through prayer, fasting, and the dismantling of evil altars, you shall unlock the doors to spiritual liberation and divine breakthrough. May your path be illuminated by His grace as you walk towards a life free from bondage.

If you're seeing this from the physical copy, type the link: <u>madueke.com/courses</u> in your browser to view all the courses on my website.

Prayer Madueke
CHRISTIAN AUTHOR

Christian Counselling

We were created for a greater purpose than only survival and God wants us to live a full life.

If you need prayer or counselling, or if you have any other inquiries, please visit the counselling page on my website to know when I will be available for a phone call.

Click or type links.madueke.com/counselling in your browser.

Let's Connect on Youtube ▶

Join me on my YouTube channel, "Prayer M. Madueke," where I share powerful insights, guidance, and prayers for spiritual breakthroughs.

Subscribe today to unlock the secrets of the Kingdom and embrace an abundant life. Let's grow together!

Click or type **links.madueke.com/youtube** in your browser.

Table of Contents

WARFARE SECTION

CHAPTER ONE

PYTHON SPIRIT

Python spirit, Cobra and serpent are all under a principality called Leviathan which is in charge of all fearful animals both in the water, air and land. Python, Cobra and serpents are messengers of Leviathan the beast, the prince of death and hell. Any covenant with him is a vow unto death. All satanic army is under the control of Leviathan. All big and small serpents of every color are under Leviathan. The kingdom of Leviathan is covered and fortified with thick darkness. Their agents always seek to control people anywhere they find themselves.

Demonic spirits follow up any plan, order or instruction given by his agents in order to bring it into fulfillment. Their words are backed up with destruction and they are not ready to compromise the words of their agents with any opposing word. The effect of their kingdom is seen almost everywhere especially in the waters. His agents are fearless and bold enough to do anything evil in the full glare of people. They attack their victims and kill them without mercy. The spirit of python or serpent in a woman causes her not to submit to the authority of her husband and she seeks to control everybody around her. They hate to submit to authority. Their head Leviathan is the only principality that a whole chapter of the Bible was given to in *(Job 41)*. Every war against God and man, past, present and future has been led and will be led by this satanic warlord, Leviathan with his messengers- python, serpents and other fearful animals.

Python is a monstrous serpent; a large oviparous snake with a forked narrow tongue which they repeatedly flick out. As they flick their tongues out, the ignorant may think they are just playing. No, but they use it to sense odor or things around them. This means that their tongues serve as an organ of smell. This is why demonic agents can program leviathan serpents to go and strike a person. They easily trace and locate their victims through odor emanating from the victims' clothes. This is why agents of leviathan operate the same way dogs do. A dog can easily identify ten different people within a family through their unique odors. So, if a stranger comes in, the dog will know that the stranger is different. Python spirit-possessed people are known for falsehood, divination and enchantment. Python serpents are trusted agent of the devil, acting more or less like the devil in nature

Now the serpent was more subtil than any beast of
the field which the Lord God had made. And he said
unto the woman, Yea, hath God said, Ye shall not

eat of every tree of the garden? And the serpent said unto the woman, Ye shall not surely die: For God doth know that in the day ye eat thereof, then your eyes shall be opened, and ye shall be as gods, knowing good and evil. Genesis 3:1, 4, 5

- The spirit of Python is a hooded snake with venomous poison which is not easily cast out or their diseases cured easily. It can resist deliverance ministers and manipulate them at times.

- Python spirit can discourage his victims from completing their deliverance program. A typical case in point is the issue of two women in my former church who came for deliverance many times but never completed it.

- His victims are limited to a certain level spiritually and physically.

- His victims do not read the Bible or interpret it very well because they oppose anything spiritual.

- His victims operate in falsehood and produce false spiritual gifts and miracles. They imitate God's actions and deeds.

- He brings false help and counterfeit lights.

- His agents offer unholy fasting and prayers to destroy God's program in the lives of his children *(Zechariah.7: 1-7).*

- He inflicts painful incurable sicknesses and diseases. Such sicknesses cause restlessness, sleeplessness and deep internal turmoil.

In addition to the above characteristics, Python spirit as one of the principal agents of Satan has remarkable evil qualities. Given these gruesome qualities which Python, serpents and Cobra possess, there is hardly anyway these arch-enemies of humankind can be sympathetic towards his victims.

Human agents of Python spirits look down on everyone and inflict fearlessness on his agents everywhere. His covenant with any human is unto death and always the superior in any relationship, dictating and giving orders. When Python spirit is programed into the sea of your life, body organs are troubled, swollen or shrunk in size.

> *He divideth the sea with his power, and by his understanding he smiteth through the proud. By his spirit he hath garnished the heavens; his hand hath formed the crooked serpent. Job 26:12-13*

Anyone possessed with Python spirit is never submissive, but make trouble anywhere they are until they get to the top in order to divert divine orders. In times of war, they rule and reign by causing anguish without mercy with the strength of lions, viper and fiery serpents.

The burden of the beasts of the south: into the land of trouble and anguish, from whence come the young and old lion, the viper and fiery flying serpent, they will carry their riches upon the shoulders of young asses, and their treasures upon the bunches of camels, to a people that shall not profit them. Isaiah 30:6

He that diggeth a pit shall fall into it; and whoso breaketh an hedge, a serpent shall bite him. Whoso removeth stones shall be hurt therewith; and he that cleaveth wood shall be endangered thereby. If the iron be blunt, and he do not whet the edge, then must he put to more strength: but wisdom is profitable to direct. Surely the serpent will bite without enchantment; and a babbler is no better. Ecclesiastes 10:8-11

Python spirit monitors God's children who err or break an hedge and they obey God's commandment to bite them without negotiating with God. While Leviathan controls and causes international wars, Python spirit monitors and causes local wars and bring his victims to untold hardship and painful sufferings.

CHAPTER TWO

ACTIVITIES OF PYTHON SPIRIT

When the Python spirit entered Cain, Abel's brother, he manipulated him to an evil field, probably a place of evil sacrifice where he talked to him, fought him and later killed him.

And Cain talked with Abel his brother: and it came to pass, when they were in the field, that Cain rose up against Abel his brother, and slew him. Genesis 4:8

He manipulated Eve, told lies against God and moved her to look at the forbidden fruits, pushed her hands to reach out to the fruits, pluck it out and eat it against God's will. Moreover, he possessed Eve, used her to deceive Adam and compelled him to break the commandment of God. Later on, when God visited them in the garden with the plan to deliver them from the bondage of the serpent, but instead of repenting, acknowledging their sins and forsaking them, they began to shift blames and claim innocent of their actions. He manipulated the marriages of the sons of God, and used their wrong marriages to bring them into wicked actions, evil thoughts and imaginations without repentance.

And it came to pass, when men began to multiply on the face of the earth, and daughters were born unto them, That the sons of God saw the daughters of men that they were fair; and they took them wives of all which they chose. And the Lord said, my spirit shall not always strive with man, for that he also is flesh: yet his days shall be an hundred and twenty years. There were giants in the earth in those days; and also, after that, when the sons of God came in unto the daughters of men, and they bare children to them, the same became mighty men which were of old, men of renown. And God saw that the wickedness of man was great in the earth, and that every imagination of the thoughts of his heart was only evil continually. And it repented the Lord that he had made man on the earth, and it grieved him at his heart. Genesis 6:1-6.

As a result, God used the flood to destroy that generation and the Python did not help them in their trouble, suffering and pains. After the flood, rather than praising and giving thanks to God for delivering them, the Python spirit manipulated them into finding fault with God and they started making plans without God. In their rebellion, they commenced building a tower to reach heaven without divine approval. In the midst of their disobedience, God confounded their language and scattered them throughout the world.

> *And the whole earth was of one language, and of one speech. And it came to pass, as they journeyed from the east, that they found a plain in the land of Shinar; and they dwelt there. And they said one to another, go to, let us make brick, and burn them thoroughly. And they had brick for stone, and slime had they for mortar. And they said, go to, let us build us a city and a tower, whose top may reach unto heaven; and let us make us a name, lest we be scattered abroad upon the face of the whole earth. Genesis 11:1-4.*

God later found a faithful man, Abraham in their midst and called him to separate himself from the crowd of sinners. In obedience, Abraham answered the call, but the devil sent a Python to attack him with anti-conception demons from Leviathan kingdom, the crooked serpent. This demonic spirit followed Abraham and his wife to their old age, but God intervened and frustrated the Python world.

CHAPTER THREE

PROBLEMS FROM THE PYTHON WORLD

In deliverance school, we term the problem from Leviathan, Python spirit on suicide mission because they can follow their victim to their grave. In the beginning, God created man in his own image, likeness, in holiness and purity because of His love for us. Man was good from the beginning, made a little lower than the angels but because of the intervention of the serpent, Python spirit by voluntary disobedience, he failed and all mankind followed suit. Every man is naturally inclined to do evil and live in sin without having any excuse before the eyes of God, but God intervened and sent his only begotten son to die for our sake and set us free. John 3:16 …Before the coming of Christ, the devil messed up marriages, took away every joy, peace and happiness but Christ came and restored it, turned water to wine and made everyone's marriage sweet again.

And the third day there was a marriage in Cana of Galilee; and the mother of Jesus was there: And both Jesus was called, and his disciples, to the marriage.

Jesus saith unto them, Fill the waterpots with water. And they filled them up to the brim. And he saith unto them, Draw out now, and bear unto the governor of the feast. And they bare it. John 2:1, 2, 7, 8

Today, many marriages have gone sore because they have chased away Christ from their homes and allowed Python spirit, the serpent into the garden of their homes. There are lots of cases of separation, barrenness, impotency, threats of divorce and multiple divorces. Moreover, many especially genuine Christians are under the attack of Python spirit and as a result, many are not married while the married are having troubles. There are cases of many adults who lived and died without getting married. Even those who managed to get married, marry their enemies, people who hate them and wish them dead. Sin is the major thing that invites demons on suicide mission with its problem, and inability to resist sin opens the door to attacks.

Submit yourselves therefore to God. Resist the devil, and he will flee from you. Draw nigh to God, and he will draw nigh to you. Cleanse your hands, ye sinners; and purify your hearts, ye double minded. James 4:7-8

If you must be free from these demonic spirits, you are expected to draw near to God after repenting genuinely through confession of sin and forsaking it and in prayers to resist the devil. Satan can attack you with or without sin and if you do nothing in terms of praying and possibly fasting, the devil will illegally still stay in your life to torment you. Though he has no right to remain because old things are supposed to have passed away, but he can through your ignorance stay put and until you resist him in prayer, he will never leave on his own. Python spirit is so wise and so may continue to torment your heart, accusing you and reminding you of all your past sins as being the reason why you still need to be punished. As a result of your ignorance, your prayer life will be disconnected and even when you pray, you pray without faith. At other times, these demons on suicide mission, the Python spirit can manipulate you through your circumstances, making you believe that your case is impossible with time. And once you believe these lies, you may continue to suffer until you are dead and buried. But even in the grave, Jesus is Lord and can make impossibility possible if only you can believe.

Now a certain man was sick, named Lazarus, of Bethany, the town of Mary and her sister Martha.

(It was that Mary which anointed the Lord with ointment, and wiped his feet with her hair, whose brother Lazarus was sick.) Therefore, his sisters sent unto him, saying, Lord, behold, he whom thou lovest is sick. John 11:1-3

The Python spirit is a monitoring demon under the direct supervision of Leviathan and its ministry is directly against believers and worse still, against sinners with great destinies. After Mary, the sister of Lazarus and Martha gave Jesus her best by anointing Him with a costly ointment and wiped his feet with her hair, everyone expected immediate blessing, breakthrough and prosperity, but the reverse was the case. The Python spirit attacked their only brother, the only male voice in the family; the source of their inheritance, the hope of their joy and the bread winner in the family. He was attacked by sickness on suicide mission attacked him, knowing that according to the tradition of Israel, Mary and Martha would forfeit everything-their father's inheritance once Lazarus died. Therefore, in order to deal with Mary and her sister for serving Christ, their Lazarus must die with sickness on suicide mission. Many genuine believers who are serving God, doing all they can to live holy go through a lot; many wonders why God they are serving keep quiet when things like these happen. Many have died in such situation and their children lose their inheritance to satanic agents, hostile relations and unfriendly friends of their parents. The question is: why do things like these happening to the righteous, faithful, holy and possibly, prayerful Christians? The reason is because of lack of knowledge and the arrows of ignorance fired against such holy servants of God. Such powers can be dismantled by continuous prayers in faith, believing that with Christ nothing is impossible even in the grave.

When he had heard therefore that he was sick, he abode two days still in the same place where he was. Then said Jesus unto them plainly, Lazarus is dead.
John 11:6, 14

Many businesses, marriages, and health and glory f believers have died due to attack from demons on suicide mission even when God did not approve of it (John 11:4). Initially, when Lazarus was attacked by sickness, his sisters came together and prayed for him and Jesus received their prayer request. When Jesus looked at the strength of the sickness, he knew that it was not a sickness unto death but a sickness that will give God glory. For this reason, He ignored the activities of the devil and decided to handle it latter. Python spirit or witchcraft kingdom has no power to kill anybody's business, marriage, health or anything here on earth, especially when it concerns believers. The only weapon they use is ignorance of the will of God, and the inability to believe in your prayers under any situation, even in the face of death. When you pray and there is a delay, it does not mean that God has not answered. All you need to do is to continue to believe and look away from all forms of impossibility. Base your prayers and faith in the word of God, not in any opposing circumstances.

> *So then faith cometh by hearing, and hearing by the word of God. Romans 10:17*
>
> *Through faith we understand that the worlds were framed by the word of God, so that things which are seen were not made of things which do appear. Hebrews 11:3*

Confess your faith upon God's faithfulness and act upon God's word (James 2:17-26; Romans 14:21). Maintain your confession throughout the battle, in the face of negative medical reports and every hopeless situation, even at the point of death (Matthew 14:25-31; Romans 14:17-25; Hebrews 10:35-39, 23). Don't allow fears, doubts, discouragement and any negative situation or circumstances make you doubt your prayers and the ability of Christ to deliver to the utmost. It is important to note that Satan, all principalities, Python spirits, serpents, cobra, the host of the witches and wizards and every occult group have no power without your cooperation. Their main weapon is to cause you to doubt God's word, accept their arrows of fear, get you discouraged and make you accept failure as your final answer and certified result. Whenever there is a record of failure in prayers, it is never from God's side because God is even more willing to answer your prayers, to heal, prosper, bless, perform signs and wonders for you more than you are willing to ask and receive from Him, if only you follow the principles of prayers above.

If any of you lack wisdom, let him ask of God, that giveth to all men liberally, and upbraideth not; and it shall be given him. But let him ask in faith, nothing wavering. For he that wavereth is like a wave of the sea driven with the wind and tossed. For let not that man think that he shall receive any thing of the Lord. A double minded man is unstable in all his ways. James 1:5-8

Now faith is the substance of things hoped for, the evidence of things not seen. Hebrews 11:1

Therefore, I say unto you, what things soever ye desire, when ye pray, believe that ye receive them, and ye shall have them. Mark 11:24

This was where Martha got it wrong and this is where many are getting it wrong today, even now. When Mary and Martha prayed, Jesus heard them but when He came up with an answer, they had no faith to receive because of the circumstance- the threats from the grave and the heavy stone of hindrance.

Jesus therefore again groaning in himself cometh to the grave. It was a cave, and a stone lay upon it. Jesus said, Take ye away the stone. Martha, the sister of him that was dead, saith unto him, Lord, by this time he stinketh: for he hath been dead four days. Jesus saith unto her, Said I not unto thee, that, if thou wouldest believe, thou shouldest see the glory of God? John 11:38-40

The demons on suicide mission, Python spirits are very weak and powerless in the face of faith in the word of God. When Jesus appeared at the grave of Lazarus, He intended to go home with Lazarus but the Python spirit entered Martha, making her doubt the ability of Christ to deliver, save and to set free after four days of burial.

> *Then they took away the stone from the place where the dead was laid. And Jesus lifted up his eyes, and said, Father, I thank thee that thou hast heard me. And I knew that thou hearest me always: but because of the people which stand by I said it, that they may believe that thou hast sent me. And when he thus had spoken, he cried with a loud voice, Lazarus, come forth. And he that was dead came forth, bound hand and foot with graveclothes: and his face was bound about with a napkin. Jesus saith unto them, loose him, and let him go. John 11:41-44*

Removing the stone means pray again. God will not keep quiet or say no this time because our prayer today is fortified with God's mercy. If you can repent, confess your sins now and determine to forsake them to follow Christ, your prayers will be answered and your Lazarus will rise up. All you need to do is to believe and confess your faith in the word of God and every Python spirit and problems on suicide mission in every area of your life will bow. By the grave of Lazarus, Jesus lifted his voice and prayed; He thanked God the father and believed that his prayers were answered even before He started praying. How did He pray? He prayed the prayer of "MERCY"; He prayed not because of the righteousness of Mary, Martha, or because of their years of service unto God's kingdom, NO! He prayed for mercy because of the people that stood by, those who must have conspired and used the power of Python, occult power or demons on suicide mission and killed Lazarus in order to deny his sisters of their father's property.

Then they took away the stone from the place where the dead was laid. And Jesus lifted up his eyes, and said, Father, I thank thee that thou hast heard me. And I knew that thou hearest me always: but because of the people which stand by I said it, that they may believe that thou hast sent me. And when he thus had spoken, he cried with a loud voice, Lazarus, come forth. And he that was dead came forth, bound hand and foot with graveclothes: and his face was bound about with a napkin. Jesus saith unto them, loose him, and let him go. John 11:41-44

Those who killed your Lazarus, business, finances, marriage, health and any good thing in your life will regret it if you repent and ask Christ to reign and rule over your life from today. All the witches, wizards, occult men, enemies of your break-through, settlement, establishment, peace, joy and happiness will see your Lazarus arise today, in the name of Jesus. Your Lazarus will come forth and every property of the dead- their grave clothes, napkin, their bondages in your feet, hands and face will be loosed to let you go, in the name of Jesus. And you that was dead, your business, health, prosperity and every good thing that was concluded dead will come forth without any grave cloth or the properties that belonged to the devil. The question is: What is God's mercy? Simply put, mercy is God's deep and tender feeling of compassion. It is the act of being compassionate, aroused by the sight of weakness or suffering. It means to bend or stoop down in kindness or loyalty to an infe-rior: to favor or bestow something on him and to be consider-ate, especially when it is not expected or deserved.

And it came to pass the day after, that he went into a city called Nain; and many of his disciples went with him, and much people. Now when he came nigh to the gate of the city, behold, there was a dead man carried out, the only son of his mother, and she

was a widow: and much people of the city was with
her. And when the Lord saw her, he had compassion
on her, and said unto her, Weep not. And he came
and touched the bier: and they that bare him stood
still. And he said, Young man, I say unto thee, Arise.
And he that was dead sat up, and began to speak.
And he delivered him to his mother. Luke 7:11-15

Mercy is to get involved in a matter beyond the rule of law in order to help the helpless and unworthy person. Grace removes guilt but mercy removes misery. Have you not suffered enough? You need mercy and grace in this program. Am not going to bother you so much with the message of Lazarus because I have written books on mercy and 100 days prayers to wake up your Lazarus, please get the details from those two books. God will break every protocol, have mercy on you and answer your prayers against Python spirit here, in the mighty name of Jesus.

In the past, Jesus by his mercy healed all manner of sickness, diseases, delivered people who were possessed with devils, lunatics and the palsy. Never forget that He destroyed leprosy, opened blind eyes, healed withered hands, fed the hungry in their thousands, destroyed fear, walked on top of marine kingdom, healed the lame, the dumb, the maimed and paid bills for his followers.

And when they were come to Capernaum, they that received tribute money came to Peter, and said, Doth not your master pay tribute? He saith, Yes. And when he was come into the house, Jesus prevented him, saying, what thinkest thou, Simon? of whom do the kings of the earth take custom or tribute? of their own children, or of strangers? Peter saith unto him, Of strangers. Jesus saith unto him, then are the children free. Notwithstanding, lest we should offend them, go thou to the sea, and cast an hook, and take up the fish that first cometh up; and when thou hast opened his mouth, thou shalt find a piece of money: that take, and give unto them for me and thee. Matthew 17:24-27

He spoke to unclean spirits, forced them to hold their peace and commanded them to come out from those they possessed without resistance. He destroyed plagues, calmed violent storms, broke chai ns of bondages, stopped the issue of blood, healed the disabled ones and made them able. He destroyed barrenness, delivered people that toiled all nights and made them CEO'S and healed impotent men.

After this there was a feast of the Jews; and Jesus went up to Jerusalem. Now there is at Jerusalem by the sheep market a pool, which is called in the Hebrew tongue Bethesda, having five porches. In these lay a great multitude of impotent folk, of blind, halt, withered, waiting for the moving of the water. For an angel went down at a certain season into the pool, and troubled the water: whosoever then first after the troubling of the water stepped in was made whole of whatsoever disease he had. And a certain man was there, which had an infirmity thirty and eight years. When Jesus saw him lie, and knew that he had been now a long time in that case, he saith unto him, wilt thou be made whole? The impotent man answered him, Sir, I have no man, when the water is troubled, to put me into the pool: but while I am coming, another steppeth down before me. Jesus saith unto him, Rise, take up thy bed, and walk. And immediately the man was made whole, and took up his bed, and walked: and on the same day was the sabbath. John 5:1-9

After that he empowered the disciples, every believer and they went about delivering people in their generation. Through Peter he healed an impotent lame man after forty years of lameness (Acts 3:1-6). Through his disciples, he healed Aeneas, raised Dorcas and Eutychus from the dead, opened the prison door for Peter and delivered Simon, a witch, sorcerer from occultism. Who is Python spirit to keep you in bondage for life when Jesus is present with all the above promises and power to deliver to the uttermost?

And Jesus came and spake unto them, saying, all power is given unto me in heaven and in earth. Go ye therefore, and teach all nations, baptizing them in the name of the Father, and of the Son, and of the Holy Ghost: Matthew 28:18-19

And these signs shall follow them that believe; In my name shall they cast out devils; they shall speak with new tongues; They shall take up serpents; and if they drink any deadly thing, it shall not hurt them; they shall lay hands on the sick, and they shall recover. Mark 16:17-18

Every believer is licensed to operate with all power, divine ability to cast out devils from every department of the devil- Python spirit, spirit of Delilah, Jezebel, serpent and Ahab and the whole creature is waiting for you to start (Romans 8:19).

WARFARE SECTION

DECREES AGAINST PYTHON SPIRIT

Every weapon of Demonic serpent, Python spirit and Leviathan in my life, I render you impotent and command you to fail in my life, in the name of Jesus. Every Python spirit in the garden of my life, your time is up; die without delay, in the mighty name of Jesus. I cut off the crawling power and the tongue of the Python and crooked serpents in my life. Blood of Jesus, speak me out of the influence of Python spirit in my destiny, in the name of Jesus.

Canst thou draw out leviathan with an hook? or his tongue with a cord which thou lettest down? Canst thou put an hook into his nose? or bore his jaw through with a thorn? Will he make many supplications unto thee? will he speak soft words unto thee? Will he make a covenant with thee? wilt thou take him for a servant forever? Job 41:1-4

With the cord and divine hook, I remove every witchcraft animal in the waters of my life, in the name of Jesus. O hand of God, destroy the smelling taste, nose and bore the jaw of the

Python in my life. I destroy every legal ground of Python spirit in my life and replace it with your divine presence the rest of my life here on earth, in the mighty name of Jesus.

> *Wilt thou play with him as with a bird? or wilt thou bind him for thy maidens? Canst thou fill his skin with barbed irons? or his head with fish spears? Lay thine hand upon him, remember the battle, do no more. Behold, the hope of him is in vain: shall not one be cast down even at the sight of him? None is so fierce that dare stir him up: who then is able to stand before me? Job 41:5, 7-10*

Let every negative utterance ever spoken against me by the agents of Python spirits be reversed by the speaking blood of Jesus. Let every negative petition or accusation against my life and destiny from Leviathan kingdom be nullified by the blood of Jesus. I break and loose myself from the covenant and curses of Python spirit and serpentine kingdom. O Lord arise and take me away from the powers assigned to terminate my relationship with God, in the name of Jesus. I break and loose myself from every relationship between me and marine kingdom. Almighty God, by your mercy, feed every Python spirit in my life with poisonous food and drinks, in the name of Jesus. I bind and cast out every evil spirit attacking my life from Python kingdom. Let any battle going on against me spiritually and physically be terminated to my favor, in the name of Jesus.

> *Thou didst divide the sea by thy strength: thou brakest the heads of the dragons in the waters. Thou brakest the heads of leviathan in pieces, and gavest him to be meat to the people inhabiting the wilderness. Thou didst cleave the fountain and the flood: thou driedst up mighty rivers. Psalms 74:13-15*

Let the judgment of God fall upon every serpent, cobra, Python and Leviathan activities in my life, in the name of Jesus. Let the waters of my life discharge every problem deposited into it by Python spirits, in the mighty name of Jesus. Let the strength of Python spirits in my life be broken to pieces, in the name of Jesus. Let the heads of the dragon, Leviathan, Python, and all serpents in my life be crushed to death. Let every organized darkness from the Python camp working to overthrow Christ in my life be disorganized forever, in the name of Jesus. Almighty God, empower me to recover every good thing I lost to

Python spirit, including the ones my ancestors lost. Let the waters within and around Leviathan, Python and the serpents in my life dry up now, in the name of Jesus.

DECREES AGAINST PROBLEMS FROM PYTHON SPIRIT

Let the venom of Leviathan, Python spirits and serpents in my life dry up immediately, in the name of Jesus. I bind and cast out every sexual demon programmed into my life from the marine kingdom. Every incurable sickness or diseases in my body from Python kingdom, receive death and die, in the name of Jesus.

And Jesus went about all Galilee, teaching in their synagogues, and preaching the gospel of the kingdom, and healing all manner of sickness and all manner of disease among the people. And his fame went throughout all Syria: and they brought unto him all sick people that were taken with divers' diseases and torments, and those which were possessed with devils, and those which were lunatick, and those that had the palsy; and he healed them. And there followed him great multitudes of people from Galilee, and from Decapolis, and from Jerusalem, and from Judaea, and from beyond Jordan. Matthew 4:23-25

Let any area of my life captured by evil spirit be released by force, in the mighty name of Jesus. Holy Ghost fire, burn to ashes every problem injected into my life by Python spirit. Let the anointing to break away from the bondage of Python spirit fall upon me, in the name of Jesus. I bind and cast out any spirit of leprosy, hatred and rejection upon my life.

When he was come down from the mountain, great multitudes followed him. And, behold, there came a leper and worshipped him, saying, Lord, if thou wilt, thou canst make me clean. And Jesus put forth his hand, and touched him, saying, I will; be thou clean. And immediately his leprosy was cleansed. And Jesus saith unto him, see thou tell no man; but go thy way, shew thyself to the priest, and offer the gift that Moses commanded, for a testimony unto them. Matthew 8:1-4

I bring every member of my family for deliverance before the Lord Jesus Christ; O Lord, deliver my family. Let every enemy against my total deliverance from hatred and rejection be exposed and disgraced, in the name of Jesus. Let the will of God for my healing, prosperity and breakthroughs begin to manifest. Lord Jesus, stretch forth your hand of mercy and compassion and deliver me wherever I need deliverance. Every enemy of my peace, joy, testimony and happiness, be disgraced wherever you are, in the name of Jesus.

Any demonic character from serpentine kingdom, your time is up; be destroyed, in the name of Jesus. Let the mercy of God manifest in the lives of every member of my family. Heavenly father, take me away from the captivity of Python spirit, in the name of Jesus. Let any area of my life that is possessed by the spirit of serpent, Leviathan and Python receive complete deliverance, in the name of Jesus. Let any Python spirit attacking me from my foundation receive destruction.

When the even was come, they brought unto him many that were possessed with devils: and he cast out the spirits with his word, and healed all that were sick: That it might be fulfilled which was spoken by Esaias the prophet, saying, Himself took our infirmities, and bare our sicknesses. Matthew 8:16-17

I command all prophesy of God for my deliverance, healing and breakthroughs to receive fulfilment now, in the name of Jesus. Lord Jesus Christ, come into my life to rule and reign forever, in the mighty name of Jesus. Every fierce demon tormenting my life, your time is up; begin to torment your own life. Every long-term problem in my life that refused to go, your time is up; go and come back no more, in the name of Jesus.

Every demon of spiritual and physical blindness, poverty and hardship in my life, I bind and cast you out, in the name of Jesus. Any part of my life under the attack of Python spirit, I command you to be delivered and set free, in the name of Jesus. Almighty God, deliver me from fear, demonic hunger, limitations, accidents, evil plans and accusations from Python kingdom, in the name of Jesus.

And it came to pass the day after, that he went into a city called Nain; and many of his disciples went with him, and much people. Now when he came nigh to the gate of the city, behold, there was a dead man carried out, the only son of his mother, and she was a widow: and much people of the city was with her. And when the Lord saw her, he had compassion on her, and said unto her, Weep not. And he came and touched the bier: and they that bare him stood still. And he said, Young man, I say unto thee, Arise. And he that was dead sat up, and began to speak. And he delivered him to his mother. And there came a fear on all: and they glorified God, saying, that a great prophet is risen up among us; and, That God hath visited his people. And this rumor of him went forth throughout all Judaea, and throughout all the region round about. Luke 7:11-17

Let every enemy of God's program, long life and prosperity against any member of my family be exposed and disgraced, in the name of Jesus. Father Lord by your mercy, let every good thing that is dead in my life, business and marriage come alive, in the name of Jesus. Let any satanic veil covering my destiny and glory catch fire and burn to ashes. Let every stone of hindrance on my way to greatness be rolled away by the power of resurrection, in the mighty name of Jesus. Every unclean spirit in my life, your time is up; hold your peace and come out of my life. Blood of Jesus, speak me out of every infirmity and deliver me from every curse, in the name of Jesus.

DECREES AGAINST POOR FINISHING

By the anointing of the Holy Spirit, I break and loose myself from the yoke of poor finishing, in the name of Jesus. Let every mountain of hindrance on my way to the end be removed by thunder from above, in the name of Jesus.

The burden of the beasts of the south: into the land of trouble and anguish, from whence come the young and old lion, the viper and fiery flying serpent, they will carry their riches upon the shoulders of young asses, and their treasures upon the bunches of camels, to a people that shall not profit them. Isaiah 30:6

He divideth the sea with his power, and by his understanding he smiteth through the proud. By his spirit he hath garnished the heavens; his hand hath formed the crooked serpent. Job 26:12-13

Let every burden brought into my life by Python spirit, Leviathan and serpents drop forever out of my life, in the name of

Jesus. Any plague, storms, evil wind that has refused to leave my life alone, I command you to disappear and come back no more. Let the fire of God enter into every area of my life and burn every yoke of iniquity in my life to ashes, in the mighty name of Jesus. I bind and cast out any evil spirit blocking my way to miracles, signs and wonders, in the name of Jesus.

Let every satanic attack presently going on against my destiny be terminated by heavenly force, in the name of Jesus. Lord Jesus, my burden bearer, take away every burden brought into my life by Python spirits, in the name of Jesus. Let the troublers of my destiny be troubled from every side until they are all dead, in the name of Jesus. Let every demonic sickness, poison of the young lion, viper and flying fiery serpent against my life and destiny perish forever. Every good thing that Python spirit has stolen from my life, I recover you double, in the name of Jesus. Almighty God, by your mercy, I take back my riches lost to Python spirit by my ancestors.

> *He that diggeth a pit shall fall into it; and whoso breaketh an hedge, a serpent shall bite him. Whoso removeth stones shall be hurt therewith; and he that cleaveth wood shall be endangered thereby. If the iron be blunt, and he do not whet the edge, then*

must he put to more strength: but wisdom is profitable to direct. Surely the serpent will bite without enchantment; and a babbler is no better. Ecclesiastes 10:8-11

Let every pit dug against me by serpents and Python of my place of birth swallow all my unrepentant enemies, in the name of Jesus. Almighty God, deliver me from every evil character that causes me to break the hedge. Let every serpentine bite in any area of my life be healed, in the name of Jesus. Every stone removed by my ancestors now hurting my destiny, I bring you back to your place, in the name of Jesus. Father Lord, restore my spiritual life and empower me to win in every battle. I receive the strength that I need to fulfil my destiny and serve my generation according to the will of God, in the name of Jesus.

Now the serpent was more subtil than any beast of the field which the Lord God had made. And he said unto the woman, Yea, hath God said, Ye shall not eat of every tree of the garden? And the woman said unto the serpent, we may eat of the fruit of the trees of the garden: But of the fruit of the tree which is in the midst of the garden, God hath said, Ye shall not eat of it, neither shall ye touch it, lest ye die. Genesis 3:1-3

Let the subtlety and wisdom of the old serpent in my life fail woefully before me in every area of my life, in the name of Jesus. Almighty God, deliver me from the lies and deceit of the serpent in the garden of my life. Every serpent or Python in the garden of my life, I cut you to pieces, in the name of Jesus. Let every influence, deceit and manipulation of the accuser of the brethren, adversary of my life, Beelzebub, dragon, father of lies, Lucifer, old serpent, rulers of darkness over my life be terminated forever, in the name of Jesus. Let the anointing to restart and finish every abandoned project in my life possess me and carry me through to the end, in the name of Jesus. Almighty God, increase my ability to be the first in every competition and to surpass my enemies and all that have gone ahead of me, in the name of Jesus.

POWER TO OVERTHROW THE ENEMY

Except God helps a man and empowers him spiritually, nobody has power close to the power of our enemy in life. Our enemies are so powerful that only God's grace when we have faith in Christ can deliver us. Unpowered people in the world are not a match to the powers of the devil who is our arch enemy.

> *Then certain of the vagabond Jews, exorcists, took upon them to call over them which had evil spirits the name of the Lord Jesus, saying, we adjure you by Jesus whom Paul preacheth. And there were seven sons of one Sceva, a Jew, and chief of the priests, which did so. And the evil spirit answered and said, Jesus I know, and Paul I know; but who are ye? And the man in whom the evil spirit was leaped on them, and overcame them, and prevailed against them, so that they fled out of that house naked and wounded.*
> *Acts 19:13-16*

Even some who professed to be Christians fail on the day of battle for failing to appropriate or use God's power. A Roman soldier would never go into battle without putting on his helmet. The helmet was prepared to protect the head from arrows and from the broad sword.

> *"And this, knowing the season, that now it is high time for you to awake out of sleep: for now, is salvation nearer to us than when we first believed. The night is far spent, and the day is at hand: let us therefore cast off the works of darkness, and let us put on the armor of light. Let us walk honestly, as in the day; not in reveling and drunkenness, not in chambering and wantonness, not in strife and jealousy. But put ye on the Lord Jesus Christ, and make not provision for the flesh, to fulfill the lusts thereof."*
> *Romans 13:11-14*

The prayers in this section will empower you to unseat the enemies of your destiny, dethrone the Pharaoh of your life, and bring peace into your entire being.

> *"And the seventy returned with joy, saying, Lord, even the devils are subject unto us in thy name. And he said unto them, I beheld Satan fallen as lightning*

from heaven. Behold, I have given you authority to tread upon serpents and scorpions, and over all the power of the enemy: and nothing shall in any wise hurt you." Luke 10:17-19

As you pray this prayer, all your known and unknown enemies will surrender. Their strength will be weakened, and their confusion will increase. Wonderful changes will begin to take place in your life and you will be promoted above your enemies.

PRAYER POINTS

1. I receive divine grace to frustrate all the enemies of my destiny, in the name of Jesus.

2. Let all my enemies sitting on the throne of power be overthrown, in the name of Jesus.

3. Power that dethroned Pharaoh, arise and fight for me, in the name of Jesus.

4. Every enemy of my peace, be overthrown by force, in the name of Jesus.

5. Lord Jesus, deliver me from known and unknown enemies, in the name of Jesus.

6. Father Lord, convert the strength of all my enemies into weakness, in the name of Jesus.

7. Holy Spirit, arise and overthrow all my stubborn enemies, in the name of Jesus.

8. I fire the arrows of death into the camp of my unrepentant enemies, in the name of Jesus.

9. Let all my enemies receive multiple confusion in the name of Jesus.

10. Oh Lord, give me wonderful changes that can frustrate my enemies, in the name of Jesus.

11. Let my prosperity cause stroke unto the bones of my unrepentant enemies, in the name of Jesus.

12. The breakthrough that will elevate me above my enemies, fall upon me, in the name of Jesus.

13. Breath of God, arise and promote me above my enemies, in the name of Jesus.

14. Oh Lord, put your power into my name to make me great, in the name of Jesus.

15. Blood of Jesus, let your power arise in anger and overthrow my enemies, in the name of Jesus.

16. Let the power that destroyed the throne of Babylon destroy all evil thrones against me, in the name of Jesus.

17. Fire of God, burn to ashes every evil throne now, in the name of Jesus.

18. Every evil foundation built against me, collapse, in the name of Jesus.

19. Every Goliath of my destiny, die, in the name of Jesus.

20. Every oppressive throne of darkness, scatter, in the name of Jesus.

21. Let every evil verdict from my enemy's backfire, in the name of Jesus.

22. I release myself from the powers of every evil throne, in the name of Jesus.

POWER TO DISCOVER THE ENEMY'S SECRETS

Without discovering your enemies' secrets, great losses can be recorded. The Lord does not want us to remain in the dark concerning the plans of the devil. We should not be ignorant of Satan's devices. David was able to plan well when the enemy's secrets was revealed to him

> *Then said Hushai unto Zadok and to Abiathar the priests, Thus and thus did Ahithophel counsel Absalom and the elders of Israel; and thus, and thus have I counselled. Now therefore send quickly, and tell David, saying, Lodge not this night in the plains of the wilderness, but speedily pass over; lest the king be swallowed up, and all the people that are with him. 2 Samuel 17:15-16*

All the secrets of the king of Syria were revealed to Elisha to frustrate his plans and save the children of Israel. When you have the power to discover the enemies' secrets, the battle of life will be made easy for you.

Then the king of Syria warred against Israel, and took counsel with his servants, saying, in such and such a place shall be my camp. And the man of God sent unto the king of Israel, saying, beware that thou pass not such a place; for thither the Syrians are come down. And the king of Israel sent to the place which the man of God told him and warned him of, and saved himself there, not once nor twice. Therefore, the heart of the king of Syria was sore troubled for this thing; and he called his servants, and said unto them, Will ye not shew me which of us is for the king of Israel? And one of his servants said, None, my lord, O king: but Elisha, the prophet that is in Israel, telleth the king of Israel the words that thou speakest in thy bedchamber. 2 Kings 6:8-12

The prayers here will empower you to see both spiritually and physically. Every yoke of ignorance upon your life will be broken. Every darkness will be cleared, and the plans of your enemies will be exposed.

Prayer Points

1. Oh Lord, empower me to do all things to glorify your name, in the name of Jesus.

2. Any yoke of ignorance upon my life, break, in the name of Jesus.

3. Every darkness around my destiny, clear, in the name of Jesus.

4. Lord Jesus, expose all the plans of my enemies, in the name of Jesus.

5. I convert the darkness built around me into divine light, in the name of Jesus.

6. Every enemies' secret against me, be discovered and be exposed, in the name of Jesus.

7. Let the stronghold of the enemy against my life collapse now, in the name of Jesus.

8. Every weapon of the enemy against my life, be destroyed by thunder, in the name of Jesus.

9. Any hidden covenant the enemy is using against my life, be broken now, in the name of Jesus.

10. Let divine touch-light flash into the dark and expose the enemies' works against me, in the name of Jesus.

11. Every generational hidden curse the enemy is using against me, die, in the name of Jesus.

12. Let the sin the enemy is using to pollute my life catch fire, in the name of Jesus.

13. Blood of Jesus, open my eyes to see every secret of my enemies, in the name of Jesus.

14. Heavenly Father, let me know what the enemies are planning against me, in the name of Jesus.

15. Holy Ghost fire, manifest in my life and let my enemies be disgraced, in the name of Jesus.

16. Let all the evil plans against me be revealed and disgraced, in the name of Jesus.

17. Every evil gang up of the enemies against me, scatter, in the name of Jesus.

18. O Lord, separate me from the bewitchment of my enemies, in the name of Jesus.

19. Father Lord, give me divine knowledge to know all the secrets of Satan, in the name of Jesus.

20. Whatever the enemy is planning against me shall fail, in the name of Jesus.

21. Let every meeting of the enemy anywhere be exposed, in the name of Jesus.

22. O Lord, take me by your hand, and reveal to me every evil plan in the name of Jesus.

I REFUSE TO SURRENDER

These prayers are for those who want to say no to their evil situations and arise above their equals in life. When you are tired of bondage, defeats, sufferings and slavery, you need to pray these prayers. If you want your name to change and your condition bettered, pray these prayers. Those who want to possess their possession and leave the life in the tail can pray this prayer and nothing will stop them from rising to the top.

And Jacob was left alone; and there wrestled a man with him until the breaking of the day. And when he saw that he prevailed not against him, he touched the hollow of his thigh; and the hollow of Jacob's thigh was out of joint, as he wrestled with him. And he said, let me go, for the day breaketh. And he said, I will not let thee go, except thou bless me. And he said unto him, what is thy name? And he said, Jacob. And he said, thy name shall be called no more Jacob, but Israel: for as a prince hast thou power with God and with men, and hast prevailed. Genesis 32:24-28

Let me tell you what will likely happen to you if you pray these prayers effectively:

a) You will end up rising above all your problem.

b) Every demonic weakness in you will fade away, and divine strength will appear.

c) Your wasters shall be wasted, and the helpers of your enemies/wasters will be eliminated.

d) When others sit, you will stand. When they stand, you will stand out differently. When they standout, you will be outstanding. When they became outstanding, you will be the standard. Nothing will be able to stop you, but you can stop all your enemies. Millions of testimonies will accompany your prayers in this section. You cannot believe what will happen by the time you finish these prayers, and your dream life will surely change.

Prayer Points

1. Father Lord, give me the power to fight to the end, in the name of Jesus.

2. Let all manner of weakness in my life disappear in the name of Jesus.

3. Father Lord, double my strength in the battlefield in the name of Jesus.

4. Every waster in my family assigned to waste me, be wasted in the name of Jesus.

5. By faith in Christ Jesus, I arise and subdue every evil kingdom in my family, in the name of Jesus.

6. By faith in the name of Christ, I overcome every environmental power, in the name of Jesus.

7. By faith in the name of Jesus, I destroy all manner of infirmities in the name of Jesus.

8. By faith in the word of God, I destroy all stubborn witchcraft attacks in the name of Jesus.

9. Hardship, I refuse to surrender to you; you must surrender unto death, in the name of Jesus.

10. Every curse assigned to waste my life, surrender and die, in the name of Jesus.

11. Father Lord, cause people to begin to honor me everywhere, in the name of Jesus.

12. Limitations in my life, surrender and die forever, in the name of Jesus.

13. Every weakness in my destiny, surrender and die, in the name of Jesus.

14. Let every satanic agent assigned to destroy me, surrender and die, in the name of Jesus.

15. Every evil pattern in my life, what are you waiting for? Surrender and die, in the name of Jesus.

16. Intimidating power of fear in my life, surrender and die, in the name of Jesus.

17. Eaters of flesh and drinkers of blood in my life, surrender and die, in the name of Jesus.

18. Arrows of wickedness tormenting my life, surrender and die, in the name of Jesus.

19. You spirit husband/wife, surrender and die, in the name of Jesus.

20. Let all my spiritual wicked relatives surrender and die, in the name of Jesus.

21. Let every uncompromising bondage in my life surrender and die, in the name of Jesus.

22. Oh Lord, arise and cause my enemies to surrender, in the name of Jesus.

23. Every enemy of my business, surrender and die, in the name of Jesus.

24. Every enemy of my marriage, surrender and die, in the name of Jesus.

25. Every enemy of my sound health, surrender and die, in the name of Jesus.

26. Every enemy of my destiny, surrender and die, in the name of Jesus.

27. Every enemy of my salvation, surrender and die, in the name of Jesus.

28. Every enemy of my breakthroughs, surrender and die, in the name of Jesus.

29. Every enemy of my family, surrender and die, in the name of Jesus.

30. Let all the water spirits/demons supporting problems in my life scatter and die, in the name of Jesus.

31. Every yoke of water spirit assigned to waste my life, surrender and die, in the name of Jesus.

32. Let the anointing of weakness in my blood surrender and die, in the name of Jesus.

33. I command every yoke of demonic setbacks in my life to disappear forever, in the name of Jesus.

34. Every power of recurring problems in my life, surrender and die, in the name of Jesus.

35. Let the strongman of unforgiving spirit in my life surrender and die, in the name of Jesus.

36. All the congregation of my spiritual and physical enemies, surrender and die, in the name of Jesus.

37. Every yoke of demonic evil appetite in my life, break and remain broken forever, in the name of Jesus.

38. Every manner of demonic impossibility in my destiny, surrender and die, in the name of Jesus.

39. Let all uncompromising curse in my life surrender and die, in the name of Jesus.

40. Every stronghold of late marriage in my life, enough is enough; surrender and die, in the name of Jesus.

41. Every yoke of barrenness in my life, break and surrender forever, in the name of Jesus.

42. Every stronghold of poverty in my life, enough is enough; surrender and die, in the name of Jesus.

43. Blood of Jesus, force every sickness in my life to surrender and be destroyed, in the name of Jesus.

44. Every promoter of untimely death in my life, surrender and die, in the name of Jesus.

45. Inherited failures of my parents, you are finished; surrender by force, in the name of Jesus.

46. Fortified powers of non-achievement in my life, collapse and remain powerless, in the name of Jesus.

47. Blood of Jesus, arise and bless me with your unmerited favors, in the name of Jesus.

48. Let all evil uncompromising sexual desires that has vowed never to let me go surrender and die, in the name of Jesus.

I SHALL NOT LABOUR IN VAIN

Judas Iscariot was among the chosen. He answered the call of God, labored with Christ with the other apostles, cast out demons, and once had his name written in the book of life.

> And the seventy returned again with joy, saying, Lord, even the devils are subject unto us through thy name. And he said unto them, I beheld Satan as lightning fall from heaven. Behold, I give unto you power to tread on serpents and scorpions, and over all the power of the enemy: and nothing shall by any means hurt you. Notwithstanding in this rejoice not, that the spirits are subject unto you; but rather rejoice, because your names are written in heaven. Luke 10:17-20
>
> Now this man purchased a field with the reward of iniquity; and falling headlong, he burst asunder in the midst, and all his bowels gushed out. Acts 1:18

He forsook all to follow Christ for many years. He labored with Christ, but all his labors were vanity.

It is a dangerous thing for a Christian to labor and suffer in vain in Christ. It would have been better for such a person not to be born at all. It is not the will of God for believers to labor in vain.

> *Therefore, my beloved brethren, be ye stedfast, unmovable, always abounding in the work of the Lord, forasmuch as ye know that your labor is not in vain in the Lord. 1 Corinthians 15:58*

In this section as you pray, the Lord will help you to reap all that you have sown in the spirit for Christ. The evil powers wasting your efforts shall die, and the Lord will give you enough grace to labor more for Christ. The powers that waste laborer's efforts will be far from you. Your due blessings, rights, benefits, and entitlement will be given to you. The Lord will rebuke your Cain, Laban, and all devourers, and you will not invest in Sodom and Gomorrah (Matthew 25:41-46).

PRAYER POINTS

1. Father Lord, thank you because it is not your will for me to labor in vain, in the name of Jesus.

2. Satan, listen to me; as I sow in the spirit, I shall reap everlasting life, in the name of Jesus.

3. Any power wasting my efforts in life, die, in the name of Jesus.

4. Blood of Jesus, anoint me to receive enough grace to labor for the Lord, in the name of Jesus.

5. Let that power that created all mankind begin to create good things in my life, in the name of Jesus.

6. Any power assigned to remove me from the garden of the Lord, die, in the name of Jesus.

7. My labors shall not be left for my Cain to enjoy, in the name of Jesus.

8. My labors shall not be wasted at Sodom and Gomorrah, in the name of Jesus.

9. Any spirit of fear that wants to deny me of my blessings, die, in the name of Jesus.

10. Any power using people to hate me so as to deny me of my blessings, die, in the name of Jesus.

11. Oh Lord, arise and rebuke my Laban, in the name of Jesus.

12. Power to reconcile with my Esau and still remain blessed, fall upon me, in the name of Jesus.

13. Powers that allowed the wife of lot to invest in a wrong place, my life is not your candidate; die, in the name of Jesus.

14. Any power that wants me to open my eyes and see my labors wasted, die, in the name of Jesus.

15. I refuse to see my labor in my children wasted, in the name of Jesus.

16. Any power that wants me to labor out of divine coverage, you are a liar; die, in the name of Jesus.

17. Let the desires of my enemies be frustrated, in the name of Jesus.

18. Any battle that will not honor God and bring my blessings, I reject you, in the name of Jesus.

19. I refuse to die the death of the unrighteous, in the name of Jesus.

20. My promotion will not be channeled to my enemy; I shall be blessed, in the name of Jesus.

21. Blood of Jesus, advertise me to the people that matter, in the name of Jesus.

22. My enemies shall not be rewarded instead of me, in the name of Jesus.

23. Any evil personality that is wishing to enjoy my labor while I suffer, die, in the name of Jesus.

24. My marriage will not keep another person happy while I am sorrowful, in the name of Jesus.

25. I shall not build for another person to inhabit, while I suffer in the name of Jesus.

26. Let God arise and reward me for my labors, in the name of Jesus.

27. Any spiritual marriage making my marriage bitter, break by force, in the name of Jesus.

28. Any power from the waters diverting my blessings, die, in the name of Jesus.

29. Any taskmaster assigned to suffer me, be frustrated, in the name of Jesus.

30. Every evil diversion working to keep me suffering, be terminated, in the name of Jesus.

31. Let every occult personality assigned to divert my blessings scatter and die, in the name of Jesus.

32. Heavenly Father, send your health into my life, in the name of Jesus.

33. Any power waiting to eliminate me immediately my blessing is about to manifest, die, in the name of Jesus.

34. Blockages at the edge of my breakthroughs, clear by force, in the name of, Jesus.

35. Any sickness programmed into my life to kill me when I need life most, die, in the name of Jesus.

36. Every arrow of death fired into my life at the point of joy, backfire, in the name of Jesus.

37. Anointing to die and be wasted when I am about to make it, fail, in the name of Jesus.

38. Oh Lord, keep me to endure and enjoy to the end, in the name of Jesus.

39. Among the people that will die in shame and regret, I count myself out, in the name of Jesus.

40. Regret and shameful death, I am not your candidate; die, in the name of Jesus.

41. Heavenly Father, bless me abundantly for all my labors, in the name of Jesus.

42. Power to do what God likes and be fully rewarded by God, possess me, in the name of Jesus.

43. Oh Lord, bless me mightily beyond my expectations, in the name of Jesus.

44. Any power that is assigned to take me away temporarily or permanently out of my reward time, die, in the name of Jesus.

45. Holy Spirit, anoint me and keep me holy unto the day of my blessings, in the name of Jesus.

46. Lord Jesus, do not allow me to die before I fulfil my destiny, in the name of Jesus.

47. Any power assigned to reposition me to wrong place, die, in the name of Jesus.

48. Any power planning to promote me out of God's will, die, in the name of Jesus.

49. Any evil assignment given to me to keep me out of God's will, die, in the name of Jesus.

50. Any evil assignment given to me to keep me out of God's blessings, I reject you, in the name of Jesus.

51. Any position given to me by the enemy to labor in vain, I reject you, in the name of Jesus.

52. Oh Lord, give me your own assignment, in the name of Jesus.

BREAKING THE YOKES
OF HELL

Apart from breaking the yoke of hell in your life, living a holy life will not be easy for you. The yoke of hell is the yoke of sin. It is a yoke that links one up to a sin that will drag such a person to hell fire at last.

> And one of the malefactors which were hanged railed on him, saying, if thou be Christ, save thyself and us. But the other answering rebuked him, saying, Dost not thou fear God, seeing thou art in the same condemnation? And we indeed justly; for we receive the due reward of our deeds: but this man hath done nothing amiss. And he said unto Jesus, Lord, remember me when thou comest into thy kingdom. And Jesus said unto him, Verily I say unto thee, today shalt thou be with me in paradise. Luke 23:39-43

Without dealing with this yoke, you can even live in the church and go to hell from there. The yoke of hell can allow you to perform miracles, signs, and wonders once you do not touch them.

You can even cast out demons and live with the evidence of demon crying out as you cast them out. The yoke of hell is very wicked and intelligent.

Not everyone that saith unto me, Lord, Lord, shall enter into the kingdom of heaven; but he that doeth the will of my Father which is in heaven. Many will say to me in that day, Lord, Lord, have we not prophesied in thy name? and in thy name have cast out devils? and in thy name done many wonderful works? And then will I profess unto them, I never knew you: depart from me, ye that work iniquity. Matthew 7:21-23

"Not everyone that saith unto me, Lord, Lord, shall enter into the kingdom of heaven; but he that doeth the will of my Father which is in heaven. Many will say to me in that day, Lord, Lord, did we not prophesy by thy name, and by thy name cast out devils, and by thy name do many mighty works? And then will I profess unto them, I never knew you: depart from me, ye that work iniquity."

You may be regarded as an apostle of Christ and a true believer. But if you fail to break the yoke of hell, you will suffer eternally in the lake of fire. Every believer must take the prayers in this section seriously. The yokes of hell promote hardship, make people to complain against God, keep victims in pride, retain them in anger, and lead them into wrong choices. We must do everything possible to break this yoke so as to be with God on earth and make heaven at last.

Prayer Points

1. Father Lord, break every yoke of hardship the enemy is using to torment me to hellfire, in the name of Jesus.

2. Every arrow of hellfire, fired into my life, backfire by force, in the name of Jesus.

3. Disobedience, you are the yoke of hell; whether you like it or not, break, in the name of Jesus.

4. Yoke of envy, assigned to drag me into hellfire, break, in the name of Jesus.

5. Yoke of complaining against God, you are wicked; break by fire, in the name of Jesus.

6. Yoke of anger that has captured my life, lose your hold by force, in the name of Jesus.

7. Yoke of wrong choice in life militating against my eternity, break, in the name of Jesus.

8. Every yoke of wickedness that does not want to release me, break, in the name of Jesus.

9. Every demonic yoke of evil thoughts defiling my mind, catch fire and burn, in the name of Jesus.

10. Every yoke of self-management against God, break, in the name of Jesus.

11. Every yoke of doubting God's word and unbelief, break, in the name of Jesus.

12. Every yoke of polygamy or polyandry attacking my destiny, break, in the name of Jesus.

13. Let every manner of lying spirit that refused to let me go die now, in the name of Jesus.

14. Let the yoke of Satan in me to covet another man's wife, break immediately, in the name of Jesus.

15. Blood of Jesus, break the yoke of murder upon my life, in the name of Jesus.

16. Every satanic oppressive yoke leading me to the path of hellfire, break, in the name of Jesus.

17. Let all satanic soldiers assigned to take me to hellfire scatter and die, in the name of Jesus.

18. Every yoke of any type of idolatry working against my eternity with God, break, in the name of Jesus.

19. Every yoke of lust of any kind assigned to destroy my relationship with God, break, in the name of Jesus.

20. Let every yoke of immorality upon my life break to pieces, in the name of Jesus.

21. Let the yoke that causes me to blaspheme God begin to break, in the name of Jesus.

22. Yoke of carnality assigned to waste my life, be wasted by force, in the name of Jesus.

23. Yoke that makes me to displease God, break and break again, in the name of Jesus.

24. Yokes that remember Egypt living inside me, break, in the name of Jesus.

25. Yoke that speaks against Moses, you will not take me to hellfire; break, in the name of Jesus.

26. Yokes that bring evil report, you will not waste my destiny in the wilderness; break, in the name of Jesus.

27. Yoke of rebellion, enough is enough; break, and lose your hold over my life, in the name of Jesus.

28. Yokes that do not commit evil but supports evil, break now, in the name of Jesus.

29. Yokes of murmuring and backbiting working against the congregation, break, in the name of Jesus.

30. Yokes that gather against Moses and God, break, in the name of Jesus.

31. Yokes that blame the leadership, lose your hold over my life and break, in the name of Jesus.

32. Yoke that smote the rock twice, you are wicked; break now, in the name of Jesus.

33. Yokes of the love of money and evil divination for reward, break, in the name of Jesus.

34. Yokes that commit whoredom and bow down to idols, break by force, in the name of Jesus.

35. Yoke of prostitution, shamelessness and madness, break, in the name of Jesus.

36. Yokes that take accursed thing, assigned to stone my destiny unto death, break, in the name of Jesus.

37. Yokes that do evil in the sight of God, break by force, in the name of Jesus.

38. Yokes of household wickedness, break and lose your hold over my life, in the name of Jesus.

39. Yokes of occultism that refused to let me go, break, in the name of Jesus.

40. Yokes that take other people's position and perform the priest's sacrifice, break, in the name of Jesus.

41. Yokes that spare Agag and the best of the sheep against God, break, in the name of Jesus.

42. Every ungodly yoke upon my life, break perfectly in my life, in the name of Jesus.

43. Yoke of Judas Iscariot working against my destiny, break, in the name of Jesus.

44. Yoke of worldliness upon my life, break, in the name of Jesus.

45. Yoke of Demas that forsake Paul, break, in the name of Jesus.

46. Every manner of evil yoke upon my life, break by fire, in the name of Jesus.

47. From today, I take the yoke of Jesus upon my life, in the name of Jesus.

POWER TO EXCEL

Many people in the world even among Christians are battling with the word, "thou shalt not excel." A lot of evil utterances and negative words have been spoken against many people.

Reuben, thou art my firstborn, my might, and the beginning of my strength, the excellency of dignity, and the excellency of power: Unstable as water, thou shalt not excel; because thou wentest up to thy father's bed; then defiledst thou it: he went up to my couch. Genesis 49:3-4

The purpose of these prayers is to wrestle you out of the captivity of evil limitations and take you to the top where God wants you to be. If you handle the prayers here very effectively, you will excel in all things.

It pleased Darius to set over the kingdom an hundred and twenty princes, which should be over the whole kingdom; And over these three presidents; of whom Daniel was first: that the princes might give accounts unto them, and the king should have no damage. Then this Daniel was preferred above the presidents and princes, because an excellent spirit was in him; and the king thought to set him over the whole realm. Daniel 6:1-3

As you pray these prayers, all the evil powers holding you down will release you. The blood of Jesus will suddenly rise and set you free, scatter your enemies, and empower you to progress above all your equals. The Lord will give you divine power to excel, and all the devourers in your life will be exterminated.

Prayer Points

1. Any power from my father's house holding me down, release me and die, in the name of Jesus.

2. Blood of Jesus, empower me to excel above all my competitors, in the name of Jesus.

3. Any evil gang up to keep me non-progressive, scatter by fire, in the name of Jesus.

4. Father Lord, give me your divine power to excel in every good competition, in the name of Jesus.

5. Oh Lord, give me the power to destroy every inherited bondage, in the name of Jesus.

6. Lord Jesus, let your resurrection power come upon me for excellence, in the name of Jesus.

7. Any power devouring my labor to limit my life, catch fire and burn, in the name of Jesus.

8. Father Lord, touch my brain with your deliverance hand now, in the name of Jesus.

9. Any witchcraft attack against my promotion, die, in the name of Jesus.

10. Father Lord, send your power into my life for promotion above my equals, in the name of Jesus.

11. The level that nobody has attained before in my generation, God take me there, in the name of Jesus.

12. Any power fighting with my angel of promotion, die, in the name of Jesus.

13. Whether my enemies like it or not, o Lord, cause me to excel, in the name of Jesus.

14. Father Lord, cause my enemies to make mistakes that will bring my excellence above them, in the name of Jesus.

15. Blood of Jesus, speak 24 hours excellence into my life till I make it, in the name of Jesus.

16. Every anti-excellent spirit in my life, die, in the name of Jesus.

17. Every satanic handwriting against my perfection, be wiped out by force, in the name of Jesus.

18. I shall live to the day of my excellence and even after in the name of Jesus.

19. Burning fire of God for my excellence, increase and increase, in the name of Jesus.

20. O Lord God of Elijah, increase my excellence and keep me on top, in the name of Jesus.

21. Every agents of the devil that has vowed to disgrace me, fail woefully; be disgraced, in the name of Jesus.

22. You the strongman in charge of my promotion, promote me or die, in the name of Jesus.

23. Higher anointing for higher excellence, possess me, in the name of Jesus.

24. Oh Lord, deliver me from every spirit of the tail and keep me delivered, in the name of Jesus.

25. Any powers that vowed that I shall not make it to the top, let fire come down, from God and consume them in the name of Jesus.

26. Every arrow of the tail fired against my life, backfire by force,

27. Any power from my place of birth that has reduced me to nothing, die, in the name of Jesus.

28. Backwardness, enough is enough; die by force in my life, in the name of Jesus.

29. Any power in charge of reducing my marks, fall down and die, in the name of Jesus.

30. You that power that refused to let me excel, die and die again forever, in the name of Jesus.

31. Lord Jesus, equip me with all manner of wisdom to make it better, in the name of Jesus.

32. Lord Jesus, make me a celebrity among the geniuses, in the name of Jesus.

33. Power that helped Daniel to excel, what you are waiting for? Possess me, in the name of Jesus.

34. Power that caused Joseph to excel, arise and possess me, in the name of Jesus.

35. Every false knowledge attacking my excellence, disappear by force, in the name of Jesus.

36. Any power stealing divine quality away from me, collapse and die, in the name of Jesus.

37. Father Lord, visit me with the anointing to excel above my teachers, in the name of Jesus.

38. Lord Jesus, begin to elevate me and keep me on the topmost by force, in the name of Jesus.

39. Any evil power that has captured my excellence, release it by force, in the name of Jesus.

40. Any spiritual armed robber assigned to steal my excellence, fall down and die, in the name of Jesus.

41. Blood of Jesus, shield me from every form of confusion, in the name of Jesus.

42. All hindrances to my spiritual excellence, be roasted by force, in the name of Jesus.

43. Whether my enemies like it or not, I must excel above all of them, in the name of Jesus.

44. Father Lord, give me unmerited favor to excel above my superiors, in the name of Jesus.

45. Among all the best in the world, O Lord, make me the best in my field, in the name of Jesus.

46. I shall arise and shine by fire by force, in the name of Jesus.

VICTORY OVER DEATH

Death is a great enemy of man that has claimed the lives of millions of souls in all nations. Death does not discriminate. It kills the young, old, rich and poor. There are many kinds of death in the world. We have premature death, death at the old age, death by instalments, and death by accident. The death that kills at the harvest time is a very wicked death.

> *"And he delivered them into the hands of the Gibeonites, and they hanged them in the mountain before the LORD, and they fell all seven together: and they were put to death in the days of harvest, in the first days, at the beginning of barley harvest." 2 Samuel 21:9*

The death that visits victims when they need their life most or after labor, and in times of harvest is a very wicked death. Hezekiah was confronted by that kind of death, but he turned to God and God delivered him.

> *In those days was Hezekiah sick unto death. And Isaiah the prophet the son of Amoz came unto him,*

and said unto him, thus saith the Lord, set thine house in order: for thou shalt die, and not live. Then Hezekiah turned his face toward the wall, and prayed unto the Lord, and said, remember now, O Lord, I beseech thee, how I have walked before thee in truth and with a perfect heart, and have done that which is good in thy sight. And Hezekiah wept sore. Then came the word of the Lord to Isaiah, saying, Go, and say to Hezekiah, thus saith the Lord, the God of David thy father, I have heard thy prayer, I have seen thy tears: behold, I will add unto thy days fifteen years. And I will deliver thee and this city out of the hand of the king of Assyria: and I will defend this city. And this shall be a sign unto thee from the Lord, that the Lord will do this thing that he hath spoken; Behold, I will bring again the shadow of the degrees, which is gone down in the sun dial of Ahaz, ten degrees backward. So, the sun returned ten degrees, by which degrees it was gone down. The writing of Hezekiah king of Judah, when he had been sick, and was recovered of his sickness: Isaiah 38:1-9

As you go into prayers, the Lord will give you power over death. Premature death will be overthrown in your family and every poison in your life shall die.

PRAYER POINTS

1. Father Lord, manifest your power and give me perfect victory over death, in the name of Jesus.

2. Let every demonic messenger of premature death assigned to waste my life die, in the name of Jesus.

3. Heavenly Father, use me to dethrone death in my family, in the name of Jesus.

4. Blood of Jesus, arise and frustrate death in my life by fire, in the name of Jesus.

5. Any power that wants to waste me in the wilderness of life, be wasted, in the name of Jesus.

6. Powers that kill with poison, lose your hold over my life and die, in the name of Jesus.

7. Powers that kill with motor accident, lose your hold over my life and die, in the name of Jesus.

8. Let the destroying instruments in the battlefield fail in my life and destroy my enemies, in the name of Jesus.

9. Thou power that kills with plane crashes, my life is not your candidate; die, in the name of Jesus.

10. Death from household enemies assigned to kill me, be frustrated, in the name of Jesus.

11. Any weapon of Cain raised against my life, backfire and kill my Cain, in the name of Jesus.

12. Any evil power that wants to kill me and keep me alive as a walking corpse, die, in the name of Jesus.

13. O Lord, deliver me from the death that comes from you, in the name of Jesus.

14. Any power that wants to kill me in sin, your time is up; die, in the name of Jesus.

15. Father Lord, anoint me for long life and righteousness, in the name of Jesus.

16. O Lord, help me to fulfil my desire and live a fulfilled live before I die, in the name of Jesus.

17. Let the smiting power of death working hard to destroy my life backfire, in the name of Jesus.

18. Father Lord, arise and deliver me from the spirit of death pursing me about, in the name of Jesus.

19. Brimstone of death militating against my life, be quenched by the blood of Jesus, in the name of Jesus.

20. Any power that has vowed to convert me to a pillar of salt, die, in the name of Jesus.

21. Any power, killing people around me shamefully, your time is up; die, in the name of Jesus.

22. Power that vowed that I should bury my children, you are wicked; die, in the name of Jesus.

23. Let the anti-male seed in my lineage be frustrated by death, in the name of Jesus.

24. Powers to confront and conquer death, possess me now, in the name of Jesus.

25. I refuse to die helplessly in the hand of uncompromising spirit of death, in the name of Jesus.

26. Let the spirit of death killing people under hard labor die, in the name of Jesus.

27. I refuse to live unprofitable life to the day of my death, in the name of Jesus.

28. O Lord, turn your sword of death away from me and give me quality life, in the name of Jesus.

29. I reverse the swords of my enemies against them. Oh Lord deliver me, in the name of Jesus!

30. All the powers and personalities seeking how to destroy my life at all cost, die, in the name of Jesus.

31. Let all the hailstone of death targeted against me be diverted back to sender, in the name of Jesus.

32. Any power assigned to kill me at midnight like Egyptians' first sons, die, in the name of Jesus.

33. Every marine power seeking to destroy my life by all means, be overthrown after the host of the Egyptians in the Red Sea, in the name of Jesus.

34. Father Lord, discomfit my enemies in the battlefield with divine sword, in the name of Jesus.

35. With the edge of divine sword, let my problems die, in the name of Jesus.

36. Any power aiming to kill me in the temple of God, you are wicked; die, in the name of Jesus.

37. Any weapon of plague that has vowed to kill me, kill your sender, in the name of Jesus.

38. Oh Lord, don't abandon me in the battlefield because of my disobedience; deliver me in the name of Jesus.

39. Let the consuming fire of God killing in the camp spare me, in the name of Jesus.

40. Lord Jesus, give me complete victory over all manner of death, in the name of Jesus.

41. Any power that wants to drive me out of the land of the living, die, in the name of Jesus.

42. Deaths under demonic torment killing gradually, receive fire and die, in the name of Jesus.

43. Any power of death seeking to subdue me, you are wasting your time, die, in the name of Jesus.

44. I refuse to be handed over to my enemies to be killed, in the name of Jesus.

45. Divine Emerald, arise and pursue my enemies unto death, in the name of Jesus.

46. Great thunder of God, thunder and discomfit death assigned to kill me, in the name of Jesus.

47. Lord, hew my enemies into pieces and deliver me from untimely death, in the name of Jesus.

48. All my unrepentant enemies pursuing me with death, die like Nabal, in the name of Jesus.

49. Resurrection power of God, arise and renew my life afresh, in the name of Jesus.

50. Death, no way! The Lord Jesus is against you. I shall not die, in the name of Jesus.

POWER IN THE NAME OF JESUS

Using the name of Jesus to pray is a great privilege in life. When you receive the power that is in the name of Jesus, you can do all things in life with ease. Though the enemy may oppose you, at the end you will win in every battle. To live in this life without the power in the name of Jesus is a great risk and a failure already in life.

> *Wherefore God also hath highly exalted him, and given him a name which is above every name: That at the name of Jesus every knee should bow, of things in heaven, and things in earth, and things under the earth; And that every tongue should confess that Jesus Christ is Lord, to the glory of God the Father. Philippians 2:9-11*

This is where all the power of God is stored. Get that power today and all your enemies shall bow. The power in the name of Jesus can take you to any level of life and keep you perfectly secure from every demonic power. As you pray these prayers, you will be empowered with the irresistible power of God.

Verily, verily, I say unto you, He that believeth on me, the works that I do shall he do also; and greater works than these shall he do; because I go unto my Father. And whatsoever ye shall ask in my name, that will I do, that the Father may be glorified in the Son. If ye shall ask anything in my name, I will do it. John 14:12-14

Every knee shall bow to those who have the power in the name of Jesus. When such people pray aright, the Lord will not say no to their prayers. Get that power today and every rebellion, enemies, and problem will bow.

Prayer Points

1. Father Lord, thank you for the irresistible power that is in the name of Jesus, in the name of Jesus.

2. Let the power in the name of Jesus appear in the battlefield for my sake, in the name of Jesus.

3. Power in the name of Jesus, what are you waiting for? Manifest and bless me, in the name of Jesus.

4. Every problem in my life, I use the power in the name of Jesus against you, die, in the name of Jesus.

5. Holy Ghost fire, combined with the name of Jesus, cut the head of my Goliath, in the name of Jesus.

6. Every emptiness in my brain, I fill you with the power that is in the name of Jesus, in the name of Jesus.

7. Any power of sin that has enslaved my soul, lose your hold by the power in the name of Jesus, in the name of Jesus.

8. I use the power that is in the name of Jesus against every sickness in my life, in the name of Jesus.

9. Let the power in the name of Jesus crush every rebellion in my life, in the name of Jesus.

10. Any good thing in my life killed by Satan, receive life by the power in the name of Jesus, in the name of Jesus.

11. Let the power in the name of Jesus confuse all my enemies in the battlefield, in the name of Jesus.

12. Every imprisoned area of my life, receive deliverance by fire, in the name of Jesus.

13. Let the name of Jesus produce everything I need to make my life comfortable, in the name of Jesus.

14. Every witchcraft attack that refuses to let me go, go by the name of Jesus, in the name of Jesus.

15. Let the name of Jesus destroy every trace of fear in my life, in the name of Jesus.

16. Let the name of Jesus increase my faith in Christ by fire, in the name of Jesus.

17. Let the name of Christ command my Lazarus out of the grave, in the name of Jesus.

18. Powers in the name of Jesus heal my blindness spiritually and physically, in the name of Jesus.

19. Let the name of Jesus Christ empower my destiny to walk on the sea, in the name of Jesus.

20. Power in the name of Jesus, take me away from satanic limitations, in the name of Jesus.

21. Oh Lord, use the name of Jesus to turn water in my life into wine, in the name of Jesus.

22. I kill every spirit of infirmity in my life with the power that is in the name of Jesus, in the name of Jesus.

23. Let my Pharaoh be confused by the power that is in the name of Jesus, in the name of Jesus.

24. Let the power that is in the name of Jesus heal my cursed hand today, in the name of Jesus.

25. Let the power that is in the name of Jesus cast out every unclean spirit in my life, in the name of Jesus.

26. Let the power that is in the name of Jesus stop me from toiling in vain, in the name of Jesus.

27. Power that is in the name of Jesus, terminate my storms of life, in the name of Jesus.

28. Let the power in the name of Jesus destroy iniquity in my life, in the name of Jesus.

29. By the power that is in the name of Jesus, I terminate my journey into late marriage, in the name of Jesus.

30. Let the yoke of witchcraft be broken by the power that is in the name of Jesus, in the name of Jesus.

31. Let the name of Jesus disgrace all the impossibilities in my life, in the name of Jesus.

32. Power in the name of Jesus, stop all manner of recurring problems in my life, in the name of Jesus.

33. By the power that is in the name of Jesus, I stop all the hardship in my life, in the name of Jesus.

34. Let the power in the name of Jesus destroy poverty perfectly in my life, in the name of Jesus.

35. Untimely death will fail woefully by the power that is in the name of Jesus, in the name of Jesus.

36. By the power that is in the name of Jesus, backwardness must die, in the name of Jesus.

37. I receive unmerited favors by the power that is in the name of Jesus, in the name of Jesus.

38. Every evil pattern in my life must die by the power that is in the name of Jesus, in the name of Jesus.

39. The spirits of rising and falling will no more attack my life by the power that is in the name of Jesus, in the name of Jesus.

40. I reject evil inheritance by the power that is in the name of Jesus, in the name of Jesus.

41. Let the power that is in the name of Jesus slap the strongman of my father's house unto death, in the name of Jesus.

42. Every water spirit problem in my life, die, by the power that is in the name of Jesus, in the name of Jesus.

43. Let the power that is in the name of Jesus terminate every evil inheritance in my life, in the name of Jesus.

44. Every curse placed upon my life shall not survive today by the power that is in the name of Jesus, in the name of Jesus.

45. I receive victory over marine witchcraft by the power that is in the name of Jesus, in the name of Jesus.

FOR PEACE IN MARRIAGE

The wine in many marriages has already finished. Families need to invite Jesus again into their marriage to convert the waters in their marriage to wine. There are alarms of war in many homes of our generation, and only Christ can silence the evil voices in homes today. If you want to live happy in life as a married person, you need to pray the prayers in this section fervently.

Who can find a virtuous woman? for her price is far above rubies. The heart of her husband doth safely trust in her, so that he shall have no need of spoil. Proverbs 31:10-11

"A virtuous woman who can find? for her price is far above rubies. The heart of her husband trusteth in her, and he shall have no lack of gain." If you desire to have peace in your home to fulfil God's plan for your life on earth, arise and pray the prayers here with all seriousness.

When wisdom entereth into thine heart, and knowledge is pleasant unto thy soul; Discretion shall preserve thee, understanding shall keep thee: Whose ways are crooked, and they froward in their paths: To deliver thee from the strange woman, even from the stranger which flattereth with her words; Which forsaketh the guide of her youth, and forgetteth the covenant of her God. For her house inclineth unto death, and her paths unto the dead. None that go unto her return again, neither take they hold of the paths of life. Proverbs 2:10-11, 15-19

As you pray these prayers, all the evil birds eating the joy of your marriage will die. Your marriage will be protected, and every yoke of marital failures will be broken.

Prayer Points

1. Any evil bird eating the joy of my marriage shall be roasted by fire, in the name of Jesus.

2. Father Lord, arise and protect my marriage from the threats of the enemy, in the name of Jesus.

3. Let the power of God destroy the arrows of marital failure in my marriage, in the name of Jesus.

4. Father Lord, frustrate every anti-peace spirit in my marriage, in the name of Jesus.

5. Let the powers assigned to sow discord in my marriage fail, in the name of Jesus.

6. Blood of Jesus, arise and speak against anti-marriage forces in my life, in the name of Jesus.

7. Any power that does not want my marriage to be peaceful, die, in the name of Jesus.

8. I destroy every spiritual weapon fashioned against my marriage, in the name of Jesus.

9. You spirit wife/husband attacking my marriage, die, in the name of Jesus.

10. Let every marriage-destroying agent in my life be disgraced, in the name of Jesus.

11. I plead the blood of Jesus over my marriage by fire, in the name of Jesus.

12. Let all demonic weapon fashioned against my marriage catch fire, in the name of Jesus.

13. Oh Lord, bring down your kingdom into my home forever, in the name of Jesus.

14. Every evil imagination of the enemies of my marriage shall fail, in the name of Jesus.

15. Let all the evil decision taken against my marriage be destroyed, in the name of Jesus.

16. I withdraw my marriage from every manner of witchcraft, in the name of Jesus.

17. Evil plan of Satan against my marriage, be destroyed perfectly, in the name of Jesus.

18. Evil designers assigned to redesign my marriage, fall down and die, in the name of Jesus.

19. Any power from my in-laws planning to break my marriage, scatter in shame, in the name of Jesus.

20. Let the blood of Jesus arise and nullify every evil decision against my marriage, in the name of Jesus.

21. I quench every strange fire burning in my marriage, in the name of Jesus.

22. Powers attacking the peace in my marriage, fall down in shame and die, in the name of Jesus.

23. All the evil altars from my father's house planning to break my marriage, scatter, in the name of Jesus.

24. Let every evil influence against my marriage be cancelled by the blood of Jesus, in the name of Jesus.

25. Heavenly Father, establish your perfect peace in my marriage, in the name of Jesus.

26. Every home wrecker aiming to scatter my marriage, be disgraced, in the name of Jesus.

27. Every curse placed upon my marriage, die completely, in the name of Jesus.

28. Father Lord, recover my marriage from the hand of the marriage destroyers, in the name of Jesus.

29. Every evil counsellor against my marriage, scatter by force, in the name of Jesus.

30. Every evil power gathered against my marriage, scatter in shame, in the name of Jesus.

31. Every evil hold on my marriage, break and loose by force, in the name of Jesus.

32. Let every conflict and hostility in my marriage be disgraced, in the name of Jesus.

33. Every arrow of marital breakup fired against my marriage, backfire, in the name of Jesus.

34. Any stranger in my marriage, you are finished; die, in the name of Jesus.

35. Father Lord, arise and re-dedicate my marriage again for peace, in the name of Jesus.

36. Let every altars of darkness attacking my marriage scatter, in the name of Jesus.

37. Every evil spirit that has vowed to destroy my marriage, be destroyed, in the name of Jesus.

38. Every unfriendly friend of my marriage, be exposed to death, in the name of Jesus.

39. Holy Ghost fire, burn to ashes every evil power eating the joy of my marriage, in the name of Jesus.

40. Any curse from anywhere placed upon my marriage, die, in the name of Jesus.

41. Any evil personality that is attacking my marriage from the dark, fall down and die, in the name of Jesus.

42. Let the spirit of unfaithfulness that is destroying my marriage die, in the name of Jesus.

43. I release my marriage from collective captivity of my parents, in the name of Jesus.

44. Oh Lord my God, arise and release my marriage from destruction, in the name of Jesus.

45. Any power, reviving quarrels in my marriage, die, in the name of Jesus.

46. Blood of Jesus, recover my marriage from collapsing, in the name of Jesus.

47. Let there be permanent peace and perfect love in my marriage, in the name of Jesus.

SENDING FIRE INTO EVIL ALTARS

Evil altar is a very dangerous place. A lot of people who are presently alive are suffering as a result of evil altars attacks. Persons, blessings, and all manner of good things are summoned and wasted at evil altars. Valuable pieces of information, destines, and people's greatness are stored in evil altars.

And Balaam said unto Balak, build me here seven altars, and prepare me here seven oxen and seven rams. And Balak did as Balaam had spoken; and Balak and Balaam offered on every altar a bullock and a ram. And Balaam said unto Balak, stand by thy burnt offering, and I will go: peradventure the Lord will come to meet me: and whatsoever he sheweth me I will tell thee. And he went to an high place. And Balak said unto him, Come, I pray thee, with me unto another place, from whence thou mayest see them: thou shalt see but the utmost part of them, and shalt not see them all: and curse me them from thence. And he brought him into the field of Zophim, to the top of Pisgah, and built seven altars,

and offered a bullock and a ram on every altar.
Number 23:1-3, 13-14

Evil altars slaughter people's greatness, exchange good for evil, behead important heads, and monitor people with demonic monitoring agents.

And Balak said unto Balaam, Come, I pray thee, I will bring thee unto another place; peradventure it will please God that thou mayest curse me them from thence. And Balak brought Balaam unto the top of Peor, that looketh toward Jeshimon. And Balaam said unto Balak, build me here seven altars, and prepare me here seven bullocks and seven rams. And Balak did as Balaam had said, and offered a bullock and a ram on every altar. Numbers 23:27-30

Victims of evil altars dream of the place of their births often, experience blockages at the edge of miracles, suffer great backwardness in life, and go through periodical failures. To deal with evil altars, we have to send divine fire of judgment to their stations.

And Moses was very wroth, and said unto the Lord, Respect not thou their offering: I have not taken one ass from them, neither have I hurt one of them. And there came out a fire from the Lord, and consumed the two hundred and fifty men that offered incense. Now they that died in the plague were fourteen thousand and seven hundred, beside them that died about the matter of Korah. Numbers 16:15, 35, 49

As you pray these prayers, God's anger will arise and burn to ashes every evil altar that is militating against your destiny. The priests of evil altars will be confused, judged, and defeated.

Prayer Points

1. Father Lord, let your anger be released upon every satanic altar, in the name of Jesus.

2. Holy Ghost fire, I send you into the altars of darkness for destruction, in the name of Jesus.

3. Let the red-hot charcoal be poured upon the evil altars of destruction, in the name of Jesus.

4. Father Lord, let your anger flow into every evil altar, in the name of Jesus.

5. I command every evil altar to open wide for fire of God to burn, in the name of Jesus.

6. I release the fire of affliction to consume every evil altar, in the name of Jesus.

7. Let the judgment fire of God burn to ashes every power of evil altars, in the name of Jesus.

8. Father Lord, pour your unbearable heat of fire into the evil altars, in the name of Jesus.

9. I send the fire of confusion to burn down every evil altar, in the name of Jesus.

10. Anything representing me in any evil altar, catch fire, in the name of Jesus.

11. Let the fire of failure consume all evil altars priest, in the name of Jesus.

12. Holy Ghost fire of judgment, arise and enter into every evil altar, in the name of Jesus.

13. Let the fire that is in the blood of Jesus consume every evil altar, in the name of Jesus.

14. I send continuous plaques of fire into every evil altar, in the name of Jesus.

15. Let the evil warmth of fire burn all evil altar priests against me, in the name of Jesus.

16. Fire of God, arise and blind all my enemies on their evil altars, in the name of Jesus.

17. Let the ears of my enemies on their evil altars close, in the name of Jesus.

18. Let the evil altar priest be confused, in the name of Jesus.

19. Oh Lord, send your raging fire into every evil altar, in the name of Jesus.

20. Let horrible tempest of fire fall upon all my enemies in the evil altar, in the name of Jesus.

21. Evil altars of darkness, receive fire, in the name of Jesus.

22. Let fire meet fire in the evil altars in the name of Jesus.

23. I send the whirlwind of fire into the foundation of evil altars, in the name of Jesus.

24. Oh Lord, rain your fire into the rooms in the evil altars, in the name of Jesus.

25. Holy Ghost fire, shock and kill every stubborn and unrepentant evil altar priest, in the name of Jesus.

26. Any unprofitable load in my life from the evil altars, catch fire, in the name of Jesus.

27. Let the tragedy sent into my life from the evil altars be diverted, in the name of Jesus.

28. Arrows of infirmity from the evil altars, be roasted by fire, in the name of Jesus.

29. Evil marks upon my life from the evil altars, be roasted by fire, in the name of Jesus.

30. Household arrows against me from the evil altars, backfire, in the name of Jesus.

31. Let all sickness from the evil altars against me be roasted by fire, in the name of Jesus.

32. Every counterfeit money sent into my account from evil altars, catch fire, in the name of Jesus.

33. Blood of Jesus, quench every evil fire burning me from evil altars, in the name of Jesus.

34. Let every satanic prayer from every evil altar be roasted by fire, in the name of Jesus.

35. Every arrow of fruitless efforts from evil altars, catch fire, in the name of Jesus.

36. Any satanic poison in my life from evil altars, receive fire, in the name of Jesus.

37. Let the destroying flood of fire arise and visit every evil altar for my sake, in the name of Jesus.

38. All evil altars against me, receive the thunder fire of God, in the name of Jesus.

39. Let the continuous burning fire of God burn at every evil altar, in the name of Jesus.

40. Cloud of sorrow mixed with Holy Ghost fire, burn every evil altar, in the name of Jesus.

41. Let the unquenchable fire of God enter into the waters for my sake, in the name of Jesus.

42. Evil altars against my life, receive the brimstone of fire, in the name of Jesus.

43. Let the concentrated acid of fire visit every evil altar against me, in the name of Jesus.

44. Fire of God, fight for me on every evil altar, in the name of Jesus.

BLOOD OF JESUS, KILL AND GO

Using the blood of Jesus in battle is a great wisdom. When every other weapon fails in the battle field, the blood of Jesus cannot fail. This blood can enter into anywhere without being restricted, questioned or confronted. It is a sure weapon of victory over every evil power.

> *And they overcame him by the blood of the Lamb,*
> *and by the word of their testimony; and they loved*
> *not their lives unto the death. Revelation 12:11*

It can kill every problem and go free without being challenged. The sacrifices of your enemies will suddenly lose its efficacy at the appearance of the blood of Jesus. No power, not even the blood of Abel can outcry the blood of Jesus. Ancestral blood sacrifice and all the bloodshed of all generations cannot stand a moment before the blood of Jesus. Those who know how to use the blood of Jesus for warfare do not lose any battle in life.

For I will pass through the land of Egypt this night, and will smite all the firstborn in the land of Egypt, both man and beast; and against all the gods of Egypt I will execute judgment: I am the Lord. And the blood shall be to you for a token upon the houses where ye are: and when I see the blood, I will pass over you, and the plague shall not be upon you to destroy you, when I smite the land of Egypt. For the Lord will pass through to smite the Egyptians; and when he seeth the blood upon the lintel, and on the two side posts, the Lord will pass over the door, and will not suffer the destroyer to come in unto your houses to smite you. And ye shall observe this thing for an ordinance to thee and to thy sons forever. And it shall come to pass, when ye be come to the land which the Lord will give you, according as he hath promised, that ye shall keep this service. And it shall come to pass, when your children shall say unto you, what mean ye by this service? That ye shall say, it is the sacrifice of the Lord's Passover, who passed over the houses of the children of Israel in Egypt, when he smote the Egyptians, and delivered our houses. And the people bowed the head and worshipped. And the children of Israel went away, and did as the Lord had commanded Moses and Aaron, so did they. And

*it came to pass, that at midnight the Lord smote all
the firstborn in the land of Egypt, from the firstborn
of Pharaoh that sat on his throne unto the firstborn
of the captive that was in the dungeon; and all the
firstborn of cattle. Exodus 12:12-13, 23-29*

This blood can visit every graveyard, every security post, and the pit of hell and deliver any captive. Even the pits of hell and earth's foundation tremble and bow at the mention of the blood of Jesus.

*And to Jesus the mediator of the new covenant, and
to the blood of sprinkling, that speaketh better things
than that of Abel. Hebrews 12:24*

Whenever and wherever this blood speaks, no evil power can stand. Try it and see. You will never lose any battle again in this life. Use the blood of Jesus, kill and go.

Prayer Points

1. Blood of Jesus, arise in your power and kill every anti-gospel spirit in my life, in the name of Jesus.

2. Blood of Jesus, arise in your power and kill every anti-spiritual growth in my life, in the name of Jesus.

3. Blood of Jesus, arise in your power and kill every financial problem in my life, in the name of Jesus.

4. Blood of Jesus, arise in your power and kill every anti-conception spirit in my life, in the name of Jesus.

5. Blood of Jesus, arise in your power and anointing, and destroy the spirit of late marriage in my life, in the name of Jesus.

6. Blood of Jesus, arise in your power and deliver me completely from poverty, in the name of Jesus.

7. Blood of Jesus, arise in your anger and kill every spirit of impossibilities in my life, in the name of Jesus.

8. Blood of Jesus, arise in your wrath and kill every demon of hardship in my life, in the name of Jesus.

9. Blood of Jesus, arise in your wrath and destroy the yoke of the devil in my life, in the name of Jesus.

10. Blood of Jesus, arise in your power and finish the work of the devil in my life, in the name of Jesus.

11. Blood of Jesus, arise in your power and kill every spirit of disgrace in my life, in the name of Jesus.

12. Blood of Jesus, arise in your power and destroy every yoke of witchcraft in my life, in the name of Jesus.

13. Blood of Jesus, arise in your power and waste all the wasters of good things in my life, in the name of Jesus.

14. Blood of Jesus, arise in your anger and kill every evil habit in my life, in the name of Jesus.

15. Blood of Jesus, arise in your power and kill every evil inheritance in my life, in the name of Jesus.

16. Blood of Jesus, arise in your anger and kill every demon of sexual perversion in my life, in the name of Jesus.

17. Blood of Jesus arise in your anger and kill every household wickedness in my life, in the name of Jesus.

18. Blood of Jesus, frustrate every work of the queen of heaven in my life, in the name of Jesus.

19. Blood of Jesus, arise and destroy every root of sickness in my life, in the name of Jesus.

20. Blood of Jesus, arise and destroy every yoke of marital failure in my life, in the name of Jesus.

21. Blood of Jesus, arise in your anger and kill barrenness in my life, in the name of Jesus.

22. Blood of Jesus, arise in your wrath and kill every spirit of backwardness in my life, in the name of Jesus.

23. Blood of Jesus, open your mouth and speak destruction to the spirit of fear in my life, in the name of Jesus.

24. Blood of Jesus, arise in your power and kill every water spirit problem in my life, in the name of Jesus.

25. Blood of Jesus, arise in your anger and kill every infirmity in my life, in the name of Jesus.

26. Any evil priest that refused to let me go, die by the power in the blood of Jesus, in the name of Jesus.

27. Any evil blood speaking against me, be silenced by the blood of Jesus, in the name of Jesus.

28. By the power in the blood of Jesus, I reverse every evil decree against me, in the name of Jesus.

29. Every anti-miracle spirit in my life, die by the blood of Jesus, in the name of Jesus.

30. Let every evil power assigned to waste my life be wasted by the blood of Jesus, in the name of Jesus.

31. Any evil covenant militating against my life, be broken by the blood of Jesus, in the name of Jesus.

32. Blood of Jesus, destroy all the collective captivity working against my life, in the name of Jesus.

33. Any curse placed upon my life, be destroyed by the blood of Jesus, in the name of Jesus.

34. Every satanic attack working against my destiny, be terminated by the blood of Jesus, in the name of Jesus.

35. Every good door closed against my life, be opened by the blood of Jesus, in the name of Jesus.

36. Every household witchcraft attacking my life, be destroyed by the blood of Jesus, in the name of Jesus.

37. Let every marine witchcraft that is fighting against my destiny perish, in the name of Jesus.

38. Blood of Jesus, expose and destroy all my invisible bondage, in the name of Jesus.

39. Blood of Jesus, kill my poverty and bless me with promotions, in the name of Jesus.

40. Blood of Jesus, kill my sorrows and bless me with multiple blessings, in the name of Jesus.

41. Heavenly father, pour the blood of Jesus to kill all my problems, in the name of Jesus.

42. Blood of Jesus, arise and kill every spirit of iniquity in my life, in the name of Jesus.

43. Arrows of immorality upon my life, die by the blood of Jesus, in the name of Jesus.

44. Blood of Jesus, in your anger kill every demonic spirit of disfavor upon my life, in the name of Jesus.

45. Every yoke of non-achievement upon my life, break by the blood of Jesus, in the name of Jesus.

46. Blood of Jesus, scatter and kill all the environmental powers against me, in the name of Jesus.

47. Every resident demon in my brain, die by the power in the blood of Jesus, in the name of Jesus.

48. Blood of Jesus, arise and kill every demon of limitation upon my life, in the name of Jesus.

49. Any spiritual marriage in my life, be broken into death by the blood of Jesus, in the name of Jesus.

50. Heavenly Father, rain the blood of Jesus upon all my enemies unto death, in the name of Jesus.

FIRING ARROWS INTO THE DARK

The kingdom of darkness operates from the dark. To effectively overcome evil powers and expose them for destruction, we must know how to fire arrows of prayers to the dark kingdom

For we wrestle not against flesh and blood, but against principalities, against powers, against the rulers of the darkness of this world, against spiritual wickedness in high places. Ephesians 6:12

When an enemy is fighting you from the dark, you need divine wisdom to overcome them. The prayers here will meet your enemies where they are. The Goliath of your destiny will not continue to hide as you use the weapons of prayers in this section

And Moses was very wroth, and said unto the Lord, Respect not thou their offering: I have not taken one ass from them, neither have I hurt one of them. And there came out a fire from the Lord, and consumed the two hundred and fifty men that offered incense.

Now they that died in the plague were fourteen thousand and seven hundred, beside them that died about the matter of Korah. Numbers 16:15, 35, 49

The prayers here also will protect you from evil arrows, blind evil spies, scatter evil altars, and burn every coffin prepared against you.

PRAYER POINTS

1. Any evil power in the darkroom of my life, receive arrow of God and die, in the name of Jesus.

2. Any evil power attacking me from the dark, receive the arrows of God and die, in the name of Jesus.

3. Let my Goliath attacking me in the dark receive divine arrow and die, in the name of Jesus.

4. Every evil bullet looking for me from the dark, backfire, in the name of Jesus.

5. Any power in the dark firing arrows of backwardness against me, fall down and die, in the name of Jesus.

6. Evil spies against me from the dark, die, in the name of Jesus.

7. Let every poverty arbitrator against me from the dark die in poverty, in the name of Jesus.

8. Any coffin spirit attacking me from the dark, collapse and die, in the name of Jesus.

9. Let every star hijacker attacking me from the dark collapse and die, in the name of Jesus.

10. All my enemies in the dark, scatter by fire, in the name of Jesus.

11. Holy Ghost arrow, locate and kill all the forest spirits attacking my life, in the name of Jesus.

12. Holy Ghost arrow, arise and kill any power in the dark that wants to kill my destiny, in the name of Jesus.

13. Let the enemies of my life in the dark receive the arrow of rain of affliction, in the name of Jesus.

14. Any witchcraft power attacking me from the dark, fall down and die, in the name of Jesus.

15. Every satanic arrow targeted against me from the ark, backfire, in the name of Jesus.

16. Any power of tragedy pursuing me from the dark, die by divine arrow, in the name of Jesus.

17. Satanic poison sent into my life from the dark, kill your sender, in the name of Jesus.

18. Let the evil prophecy against me from the dark be fulfilled against my enemies, in the name of Jesus.

19. Any power distributing shame into my life from the dark, receive shame, in the name of Jesus.

20. Every arrow of infirmity fired against me from the dark, backfire, in the name of Jesus.

21. Any power arresting my finances from the dark, release it and die, in the name of Jesus.

22. Every household arrow fired at me from the dark, I fire you back in the name of Jesus.

23. Any satanic program against me from the dark, die, in the name of Jesus.

24. Every evil plantation in my life from the dark, come out and die, in the name of Jesus.

25. Any power from the dark that has arrested me, release me and die in the name of Jesus.

26. Every occult arrow fired against me from the dark, backfire, in the name of Jesus.

27. Blood of Jesus, cleanse every evil arrow against me from the dark, in the name of Jesus.

28. Any evil thing transferred into my life from the dark, backfire, in the name of Jesus.

29. I silence every evil report against me from the dark, in the name of Jesus.

30. Any agent of Satan attacking me from the dark, fall down and die, in the name of Jesus.

31. Every iron-like curse placed upon me from the dark, break, in the name of Jesus.

32. Let every marriage killer attacking my marriage from the dark die, in the name of Jesus.

33. Every evil covenant holding me from the dark, break by force, in the name of Jesus.

34. Spirit wife/husband from the dark, fall down and die, in the name of Jesus.

35. Owners of evil load against me from the dark, carry your load, in the name of Jesus.

36. Every arrow of late progress fired into my life from the dark, backfire, in the name of Jesus.

37. Evil money sent into my money from the dark, catch fire and burn, in the name of Jesus.

38. Any manipulators, manipulating me from the dark, collapse and die, in the name of Jesus.

39. Any idol of my father's house attacking my life, scatter and die, in the name of Jesus.

40. Every satanic prayer warrior praying against me, scatter in shame, in the name of Jesus.

41. Any angel of darkness following me about, you are finished; die, in the name of Jesus.

42. Every secret oppressor, oppressing me from the dark, be oppressed unto death, in the name of Jesus.

43. Every garment of poverty upon me from the dark, catch fire and burn, in the name of Jesus.

44. Any part of my destiny in the dark, come out by force, in the name of Jesus.

45. Every manner of evil arrow ever fired against me from the dark, backfire, in the name of Jesus.

PRAYING FOR DIVINE MERCY

The scarcity of divine mercy anywhere brings mass destruction. Lack of divine mercy enables the devil to work and destroy without restriction. Our generation needs divine mercy more than ever before. Lack of divine mercy on earth exposes people to satanic attacks

Have mercy upon me, O God, according to thy lovingkindness: according unto the multitude of thy tender mercies blot out my transgressions. Wash me thoroughly from mine iniquity, and cleanse me from my sin. For I acknowledge my transgressions: and my sin is ever before me. Against thee, thee only, have I sinned, and done this evil in thy sight: that thou mightiest be justified when thou speakest, and be clear when thou judgest. Behold, I was shapen in iniquity; and in sin did my mother conceive me. Psalms 51:1-5

Without divine mercy, believers will go out of divine coverage and die without help. As you pray for divine mercy in this program, the Lord will turn His anger away from you. He will eliminate every confusion and the activities of household wickedness in your life. Pray this prayer and God will anoint you for divine mercy and unmerited favours.

Prayer Points

1. Father Lord, forgive me for leaving you to the camp of my enemy, in the name of Jesus.

2. Oh Lord, by your divine mercy, deliver me from the captivity of the devil, in the name of Jesus.

3. Lord Jesus, by the power of your all grace, deliver me now, in the name of Jesus.

4. Let my destiny be set free by the great grace of God, in the name of Jesus.

5. Father Lord, by your manifold grace, arise and set me free, in the name of Jesus.

6. Abundant grace of God, appear and manifest in my life, in the name of Jesus.

7. Let God's exceeding grace take me away from demonic coverage area, in the name of Jesus.

8. Oh Lord, by your mercy, deliver me from the grief of witchcraft, in the name of Jesus.

9. Lord Jesus, by your mercy, turn your anger away from me, in the name of Jesus.

10. Father Lord, I plead for your mercy; deliver me from confusion, in the name of Jesus.

11. Anointing for divine mercy, fall upon me and deliver me from household wickedness, in the name of Jesus.

12. By divine mercy, I break out from every bondage of poverty, in the name of Jesus.

13. Divine mercy, arise and set me free from the arrest of the spirit of tragedy, in the name of Jesus.

14. Father Lord, don't allow me to die out of coverage area, in the name of Jesus.

15. Any power that wants me to die in reproach, fail woefully now, in the name of Jesus.

16. Every yoke of failure in my life, break by divine mercy, in the name of Jesus.

17. Any power that has vowed to keep me in life's prison, release me now, in the name of Jesus.

18. Any problem that has captured me, you are a liar; die now, in the name of Jesus in the name of Jesus.

19. Oh Lord, deliver me from the hand of my tormentors, in the name of Jesus.

20. By divine mercy, oh Lord, deliver me from my family idol, in the name of Jesus.

21. By divine mercy, Oh Lord, deliver me from late progress, in the name of Jesus.

22. Every bondage of evil inheritance, break by divine mercy, in the name of Jesus.

23. Let the mercy of God set me free form the captivity of every evil, in the name of Jesus.

24. By divine mercy, I command the strongman of my father's house to die, in the name of Jesus.

25. Every yoke of poverty in my life, break by divine mercy, in the name of Jesus.

26. Heavenly Father, break the yoke of fear upon my life, in the name of Jesus.

27. Impossibilities in my life, disappear and let possibilities appear, in the name of Jesus.

28. Let the divine mercy of God break every yoke of non-achievement in my life, in the name of Jesus.

29. Any power that wants me to die in Egypt, die, in the name of Jesus.

30. Oh Lord, hold my marriage by your mercy forever, in the name of Jesus.

31. Every yoke of sickness in my life, break by divine mercy, in the name of Jesus.

32. Every yoke of hardship in my life, break by divine mercy, in the name of Jesus.

33. Every yoke of the water spirit in my life, break by divine mercy, in the name of Jesus.

34. By divine mercy, I shall arise again by force, in the name of Jesus.

35. Blood of Jesus, renew my life and prosper me by divine mercy, in the name of Jesus. In the name of Jesus.

36. Every spirit of failure in my life, die and perish by divine mercy, in the name of Jesus.

37. By divine mercy, let my eagle fly high, in the name of Jesus.

38. Oh Lord, use your divine mercy to promote my expired destiny, in the name of Jesus.

39. Any power that has vowed to bring me to square one, die by divine mercy, in the name of Jesus.

40. Divine mercy, take me from where I am now to where you want me to be, in the name of Jesus.

41. I shall walk back to my original by divine mercy, in the name of Jesus.

42. Oh Lord, assist me to recover all my lots by divine mercy, in the name of Jesus.

THANK YOU!

I'd like to use this time to thank you for purchasing my books and helping my ministry and work. Any copy of my book you buy helps to fund my ministry and family, as well as offering much-needed inspiration to keep writing. My family and I are very thankful, and we take your assistance very seriously.

You have already accomplished so much, but I would appreciate an honest review of some of my books through the link below. This is critical since reviews reflect how much an author's work is respected.

Please [click here] to leave a review on Amazon. If you're viewing from a printed version, please visit amazon.com/review/create-review?asin=B08VBH5P4V to leave a review.

Please be aware that I read and value all comments and reviews. You can always post a review even though you haven't finished the book yet, and then edit your reviews later.

Thank you so much as you spare a precious moment of your time and may God bless you and meet you at the very point of your need.

You can also send me an email to hello@madueke.com if you encounter any difficulty while writing your review.

PRAYER M. MADUEKE'S BESTSELLING BOOKS

Click on any of the [Buy Now] buttons to view or purchase them on my website. If you're viewing from a printed version, please visit madueke.com and search for these books.

1. Dictionary of Demons & Complete Deliverance [Buy Now]

2. Monitoring Spirits [Buy Now]

3. Praying with The Blood of Jesus [Buy Now]

4. The Power of Speaking in Tongues [Buy Now]

5. Speaking Things into Existence by Faith [Buy Now]

6. Discerning and Defeating the Ahab & Jezebel Spirit [Buy Now]

7. Defeating the Python Spirit [Buy Now]

8. 35 Special Dangerous Decrees [Buy Now]

9. 21/40 Nights of Decrees and Your Enemies Will Surrender [Buy Now]

10. Command the Morning, Day and Night [Buy Now]

11. Evil Summon [Buy Now]

12. Overcoming & Destroying the Spirit of Rejection & Hatred [Buy Now]

13. Queen of Heaven: Wife of Satan [Buy Now]

14. The False Prophet [Buy Now]

15. Dominion Over Sickness & Disease [Buy Now]

16. The Battle Plan for Destroying Foundational Witchcraft [Buy Now]

17. The Queen of the Coast [Buy Now]

18. Dictionary of Unmerited Favor [Buy Now]

19. Prayers for Breakthrough in your Business [Buy Now]

20. A Jump From Evil Altar [Buy Now]

21. 100 Days Prayers to Wake Up Your Lazarus [Buy Now]

22. Breaking Evil Yokes [Buy Now]

23. When Evil Altars are Multiplied [Buy Now]

24. The Battle Plan for Destroying
    Foundational Occultism   [Buy Now]

25. Prayers for Protection   [Buy Now]

26. Prayers for Academic Success   [Buy Now]

27. Your Dream Directory   [Buy Now]

28. Prayers for Financial Breakthrough   [Buy Now]

29. Destiny and Star Hunters   [Buy Now]

30. Prayers to Pray during Courtship   [Buy Now]

31. 91 Days Decrees to Takeover the Year   [Buy Now]

32. Alone with God   [Buy Now]

33. Prayers against Satanic Oppression   [Buy Now]

34. Foundations Exposed   [Buy Now]

35. Prayers for Deliverance   [Buy Now]

36. Prayers to Heal Broken Relationship   [Buy Now]

37. Prayers for Good Health   [Buy Now]

38. Comprehensive Deliverance [Buy Now]

39. Prayers for College and University Students [Buy Now]

40. 40 Prayer Giants [Buy Now]

41. Divine Protection & Immunity While Sleeping [Buy Now]

42. Prayers for Fertility in your Marriage [Buy Now]

43. More Kingdoms to Conquer [Buy Now]

44. Confront and Conquer your Enemy [Buy Now]

45. Prayers to Raise Godly Children [Buy Now]

4 Free Ebooks

In order to say a 'Thank You' for purchasing *Defeating the Python Spirit*, I offer these books to you in appreciation. Click or type maer browser.maueke.com/free-gift in your browser.

Video Bonus

I've created exclusive video content to complement the topics covered in the book. These videos provide deeper insights and discussions on the things discussed in this book, offering you a more immersive learning experience.

To access the video bonus for this course, simply click or type links.madueke.com/22DPS in your browser.

Message from the Author

I want to see you succeed, grow, and break free from negativity and obstacles. My hope is for you to thrive, unaffected by negative influences and challenging situations. Because of that, please permit me to introduce two courses that I believe passionately will help you:

1. To break the evil altars and powers of your father's house, The role of altars in the realm of existence is very key because altars are meeting places between the physical and the spiritual, between the visible and the invisible.

   Unless a man cuts off the evil flow from the power of his father's house, he will not fulfil his destiny. Click here to learn more about my course on how to tear down unholy altars and close the enemy's entryways into your life!

2. To help you seamlessly break iron-like problems, illness, delayed marriage, poverty, or any long-standing battle.

   Discover the transformative power of Christian fasting and prayer. Remember, Matthew 17:21 teaches us, *"But this kind of demon does not go out except by prayer and fasting."* Ready to overcome your struggles? Click here to learn more about this course.

Embrace the journey ahead with faith, for through prayer, fasting, and the dismantling of evil altars, you shall unlock the doors to spiritual liberation and divine breakthrough. May your path be illuminated by His grace as you walk towards a life free from bondage.

If you're seeing this from the physical copy, type the link: **madueke.com/courses** in your browser to view all the courses on my website.

Prayer Madueke
CHRISTIAN AUTHOR

Christian Counselling

We were created for a greater purpose than only survival and God wants us to live a full life.

If you need prayer or counselling, or if you have any other inquiries, please visit the counselling page on my website to know when I will be available for a phone call.

Click or type links.madueke.com/counselling in your browser.

Let's Connect on Youtube ▶

Join me on my YouTube channel, "Prayer M. Madueke," where I share powerful insights, guidance, and prayers for spiritual breakthroughs.

Subscribe today to unlock the secrets of the Kingdom and embrace an abundant life. Let's grow together!

Click or type links.madueke.com/youtube in your browser.

An Invitation to Become a Ministry Partner

I appreciate the support and inquiries I have received regarding collaboration with my ministry. Your prayers and dedication to the work of the Kingdom are highly valued.

You can also visit the donation page on my website if you would like to contribute or learn more about supporting my ministry: madueke.com/donate.

Thank you for your continued support and faithfulness in Christ Jesus.

www.ingramcontent.com/pod-product-compliance
Lightning Source LLC
Chambersburg PA
CBHW021642120626
46545CB00002B/661